Security Operations Center - SIEM Use Cases and Cyber Threat Intelligence

ARUN E THOMAS

Acknowledgements:

I would like to express my gratitude to the many people who helped me to write this book; to all those who provided support, talked things over, read, wrote, offered comments, allowed me to quote their remarks and assisted in the editing, proofreading, and design. Many people helped me to make this a success and I have to thank them for aiding me in this endeavor.

Special thanks to Mr. Renjith Gopalakrishnan - without you, this book would never find its way to the Web. I would like to thank Mr. Mufeed Ubaid for helping me in the process of selection and editing. Thanks to Mr. Sudheer Elayadath my partner and co-founder of NetSentries and GreenSentries for encouraging me.

About the Author

Arun E Thomas

With over 16 years of experience as Information Security Professional, Arun holds Multiple Information Security patents and 28+ Professional IT certifications including CISSP concentrations, SSCP, CASP, ECSA/LPT and CCSE. He is the author of several books and is the Chief Security Architect & CTO of NetSentries Technologies (UAE and India) and CISO of GreenSentries DMCC. Arun holds his dual Engineering Degree from Institution of Engineers (India) and has held a number of positions during his professional career including Chief Security Architect, CTO, SOC SME, Security Analyst, Consultant and Security Practice Lead.

Technical Editor

Renjith Gopalakrishnan

An Enterprise Architect and Technology Evangelist with 13 years of success leading all phases of IT and Security projects and designing diverse portfolio of solutions. Renjith holds numerous professional IT certification including PRINCE2, COBIT, TOGAF, ITILv3, SE1 (Splunk) and other technical certification credentials. He holds a Bachelor's degree in Computer Science and Executive MBA in IT. Known for designing usable solutions understanding the business and its requirements with customer satisfaction as a priority and carry the experience of understanding what business/various stakeholder's demands from ITaaS (IT as a Service) and Security services. He is Director – Customer Success at NetSentries Technologies and GreenSentries DMCC, and experienced in Infrastructure and Security Architecture Design, Enterprise Architecture Design, Service Delivery Management, Infrastructure Management, Solution Designing, Security Project Management and Systems Integrations.

Foreword

I'm deeply honored to write this foreword for "Security Operations Center - SIEM Use Cases and Cyber Threat Intelligence" by Arun Thomas, a close friend, business partner and colleague for several years. This is the 6th in a series of publications from Arun about Threat Management in the Enterprise.

Arun is a technologist, author, speaker, inventor and a prominent personality in the Information Security industry across the EMEA. He is an active proponent of open source technologies for addressing the emerging wave of IT, IoT and Industrial Control Systems security threats.

It is clear, from the recent security breaches experienced by large and seemingly impenetrable enterprises, that attackers are more sophisticated than ever and even the most vigorously implemented and operated traditional cyber defense programs cannot defend against targeted cyber threats. Highly innovative and constantly evolving strategies are the need of the hour to defend against threat actors in today's cyber war.

The term "Cyber Threat Intelligence" has gained considerable interest in the Information Security community over the past few years. The main purpose of implementing a Cyber threat intelligence (CTI) program is to prepare businesses to gain awareness of cyber threats and implement adequate defenses before disaster strikes. Threat Intelligence is the knowledge that helps Enterprises make informed decisions about defending against current and future security threats.

This book is a complete practical guide to understanding, planning and building an effective SOC with Cyber Threat Intelligence program within an organization. Arun breaks down the components of threat intelligence and places them within the realms of understanding of general IT Professionals. This book is a must read any Security or IT professional with mid to advanced level of skills. The book provides insights that can be leveraged on in conversations with your management and decision makers to get your organization on the path to building an effective CTI program.

Happy Reading!

Sudheer Elayadath
Director, NetSentries Technologies
Dubai, UAE

MODULE 10 - THREAT INTELLIGENCE COLLECTION AND ANALYSIS

Introduction

Security analytics can be defined as the process of continuously monitoring and analyzing all the activities in your enterprise network to ensure a minimal number of occurrences of security breaches. A Security Analyst is the individual that is qualified to perform the functions necessary to accomplish the security monitoring goals of the organization. This book is intended to improve the ability of a security analyst to perform their day to day work functions in a more professional manner. Deeper knowledge of tools processes and technology is needed for this.

A firm understanding of all the domains of this book is going to be vital in achieving the desired skill set to become a professional security analyst. The goal of this book is to address the problems associated with the content development (use cases and correlation rules) of SIEM deployments.

1. The Security Operation Center Fundamentals domain details the much-needed basics one should know about a Security Operation Center. The key areas of knowledge include:

    - Security Operations Center Fundamentals
    - SOC Challenges
    - Regulatory compliance requirements

- SOC Services
- SOC Roles and Teams
- SOC Topology
- SOC Reports
- In-House SOC vs Outsourced SOC
- Outsourced SOC – Service level agreements
- SOC Analyst – Desired Skill Set
- SOC Roles
- Information Needed by SOC Roles

The ability to understand security operation Tools, Processes, Roles and Responsibilities of SOC professionals are all key elements that go into this domain.

2. SIEM deployment domain addresses the processes and steps involved in selection and deployment of an SIEM solution for the enterprise.

The key area of knowledge includes:

- SIEM Selection and Deployment
- SIEM Tools
- Types of Reports
- SOC Metrics
- How to Select SIEM
- Collector to source communication Protocol
- Challenges or Risks in Building a SOC

Proper understanding of processes and technology related to SIEM helps security professionals in designing and deploying security monitoring solutions in a very effective way. The security analyst is responsible for security threat detection to all levels based on the solution they implement.

3. MSSP SLA domain is meant for making a securing analyst understand the means, components and terms of an MSSP SLA through a sample service level agreement. This includes an oversight of the common terms and criteria included in an SLA.

4. The Network Security Monitoring domain focuses on the deeper packet or stream level analysis of data. Network security monitoring is a collection of different publically available tools for the deeper analysis of network traffic. The tools and techniques used for building and operating an NSM internally for your organization is described in detail.

The key areas of knowledge include:

- Network Security Monitoring
- NSM Deployment
- NSM Limitations
- NSM Data Types
- NSM Deployment

- NSM Deployment models
- Commonly used Tools for building NSM

5. The Recommended Use Cases and Correlation Rules domain deals with the selection of proper use cases and correlation rules. The effectiveness of security monitoring is based purely on the strength of deployed use cases and correlation rules. Event sources are categorized in to a number of categories based on their type, and a list of minimum recommended use cases and correlation rules are suggested.

The key areas of knowledge include:

Recommended use cases correlation rules for;

- Anti-spam
- Anti-virus
- End point threat protection/ Application control/whitelisting solution
- Web/Application server or database
- Data loss prevention /File integrity monitor
- Financial application
- Host based firewall
- Single sign on
- IPS/IDS

- Network based firewall
- Network user behavior analysis
- Operating system
- Storage
- VPN
- Vulnerability Scanning solution
- NAC solution

Module 1
Security Operations Center
Fundamentals

Why do we need a SOC?

The Security Operations Center plays a significant role in real time detection of threats and post threat response. There are several tools and solutions that are in use in SOC environments. This book will take you through all the must know SOC technologies and tools. The Security Operation Center is the place where all network devices, security solutions, applications and database systems are monitored. SOC also deals with the periodic assessment of threats through the use of vulnerability management tools, network security monitoring solutions, and continuous security monitoring products. End point security management, Incident Response, compliance monitoring etc. are also the other major functions of the Security Operations Center team.

SOC Challenges

There are several challenges in security monitoring, in the following section you will find more details about it.

Amount of Data

SOC tools must have the capability to handle tons of data from disparate systems, platforms, and applications. Security monitoring solutions will be acting as the collection and aggregation points of logs, the huge amount of data collection should not create any performance or throughput issues. Performance issues may directly result in interruption of monitoring services or SLA violations in case of MSSPs. The lack of raw or indexed logs will result in compliance violations. So it is extremely important to select the throughput and efficiency of SOC solutions before selecting and deploying it in your SOC.

Log rate limiting is a common practice security practitioners follow to reduce the amount of logs getting aggregated in SOC collection points, Log managers or SIEM collection points. Log rate limiting polices limit the number of logs generated at the event source itself. This ensures effective utilization of your SIEM's Events Per Second (EPS) based license.

However, rate limiting is not always priority driven. Most of the network security vendors do not offer selective rate limiting. This means you may miss highly critical logs due to the implementation of log rate limiting.

Along with rate limiting, organizations may also have control over the type or class of logs generated by the security systems. For example, Cisco IOS gives an option to selectively generate logs. Example -1 Shows the log rate limiting policy configuration in a Cisco Router.

Example -1

```
Router#configure terminal
Enter configuration commands, one per line.  End
with CNTL/Z.
Router(config)#logging host 10.10.11.14
Router(config)#logging    rate-limit    20    except
warnings
Router(config)#end
Router#
```

In the above example logging rate-limit configuration command limits the number of syslog packets sent to the syslog server to 20 events per second. In this case, it is a selective rate limiting configuration as the policing is not applicable for "warning" category logs.

Numerous End-points and Billions of Logs

Several sets of network infrastructure and security devices are in place in enterprise networks, all of these products generate logs, moreover thousands of end users get connected to the corporate network over wireless or mobile networks. The present security controls do not count the peer to peer communication between connected wireless or cellular end points. The recent developments in networking like SDN - Software Defined Networking is slowly redefining the network infrastructure architecture itself. This brings in a need for revised Information Security Policy or Logging configuration. Organizations are increasingly using cloud deployed instances or applications, most of these applications are business critical, so are the logs generated by them.

Sophisticated Attacks

It is quite difficult to initially detect the modern day sophisticated attacks just by monitoring, collecting and correlating the logs generated by different end points. Most of the time the characteristics of the threat will be identified only by deep post threat analysis.

For Example, Detection of "Lateral Movements" of an Advanced Persistent Threat (APT), needs cross correlation of multiple logs from different event sources.

Regulatory Compliance Requirements

Compliance standards mandate retention of security data. The log archiving should be in such a way that it is easy for the auditors to go back to logs from previous years to trace security breaches. The type of the security data needed, penalties for non-compliance and the minimum retention period vary per regulations.

No organization will be interested in taking the risk of not retaining logs as per the compliance requirements. Non-compliance may result in huge monetary fines and civil or executive liability, moreover having the organizations name associated with a security breach will affect the trust association it has with the customers and the existence of the business itself.

The below table lists the retention requirements of different compliance standards.

Regulatory Standard	Retention Period
SOX	7
PCI-DSS	1
GLBA	6
EU Data Retention Directive	2
Base II	7
HIPPA	6 or 7
NERC	3
FISMA	3

Table 1 Regulatory / Compliance Standards and Retention Periods

SOC Services

SOC functions seven days a week, 24 hours in a day. Typical services offered by SOC are,

- Continuous Threat monitoring and Incident Detection

- Incident Response
- Threat Mitigation
- Rule/Signature updates
- Threat Intelligence Integration
- Vulnerability Assessment
- Web Application Scanning
- Compliance Monitoring
- Managed Devices

Continuous Threat Monitoring and Incident Detection

Continuous Threat monitoring and Incident Detection - This is achieved with the monitoring of SIM/SIEM consoles, IPS/IDS consoles, AV/AS/UTM consoles and DLP/SIV/Endpoint security consoles.

Incident Response

It includes preliminary incident response, isolation of threats and coordination of different functional teams responsible for threat mitigation. Incident response is one of the major functions of the Security Operations Team.

Threat Mitigation

Most of the time SOC team members play a significant role in threat mitigation, they also do the necessary checks needed to make sure that the vulnerability or loophole is completely eradicated. SOC team members may suggest changes to existing security controls for eradication of threat and may also perform re-evaluation of threat with custom scripts or vulnerability management tools.

Rule/Signature Updates

IPS/IDS, End-point security, and Firewall rules are normally updated by SOC. In some organizations, OS and Application patch management is also performed by the Security Operations Center team. Custom signature development, retuning of the signatures and revoking of signatures in use may also be a function of the Security Operations Center team.

Threat Intelligence Integration

Integration of threat intelligence feeds with existing SIM/SIEM, perimeter security appliances like firewall and content filtering solutions is one of the prime responsibilities of the SOC team. Nowadays many of the organizations are opting for their own Threat Intelligence Platform that can consume feeds from different threat intelligent providers.

The SOC SME is usually responsible for the generalization of the data received from different threat intelligence providers. SOC resources use this intelligence to identify new attacks in time and also for reconfirmation of identified threat.

Constituency

Constituency is a term used in SOC to represent a set of customers to whom SOC provides services, these includes users, sites, information technology assets, clients, partners and organizations. A typical SOC will collect billions of security events every day, the processing power, throughput, storage space needed for the analysis and storage of security events is huge. Committee on Natural Security Systems defines an event as "Any observable occurrence in a system and or network events sometimes provides indications that an incident is occurring."

SOC Roles and Teams

A typical SOC will have multiple levels of teams performing one specific or different tasks.

TIER – 1 team is responsible for real time monitoring of security events and they also attend phone calls from clients or users related to security incidents along with other routine tasks.

The TIER – 1 security monitoring team converts alerts to a CASE based on the default threshold settings and escalate it to TIER -2. Usually the threshold level is defined based on the category and severity of the incidents, criticality of the application or resource involved in, the business impact it may have etc.

Tier-1 team only does the basic analysis of the event and doesn't hold the event with them for more than thirty minutes. Again, the process of escalation will be as per corporate /MSSP SOC escalation policy requirements, expertise of the team members involved. Event volume etc. also plays a significant role in this process. Escalation is done by Tier-1 team also to prevent the chances of missing other relevant security events.

Tier-2 team is responsible for in-depth analysis of the security events. It may take a few hours to even weeks for them to do the deep analysis. There may be multiple levels of teams above Tier-2, the incidents will be escalated to them in order if the situation demands. Tier-2 is also responsible for coordinating the post incident's actions with the constituency. Before involving the constituency, they are supposed to do the necessary checks needed for determining the relevancy of the event. For a relevancy check the Tier-2 team trusts the application / system criticality data (documents with a description of how relevant a particular asset or application is to the organization), the data available from vulnerability management solution, adversary information provided by commercial/open source threat intelligence providers.

Information provided by the partners/manufacturers of the product, history of similar kinds of threats that have happened in the past and other documented data like the response time in Service Level Agreement(SLA) are considered for the process of escalation. Incidents may be associated with hundreds to thousands of security events. Recovery from an incident usually demands participation of internal and external experts. Forensic analysis or malware analysis may be performed based on the nature and behavior of the threat. Proper consumption of Cyber Threat Intelligence (CTA), equips the SOC team to properly define and execute response actions. Centralized monitoring for detection of threats in a timely manner and continuous prevention are the major goals/objectives of the SOC. The properly defined and deployed SOC helps the organization to react to threats in a faster way. In fact, every millisecond is important in identifying and preventing threats before they can cause damage.

Modern day SOC aids computer forensics with not only the centralized collection or aggregation of logs, but by offering a platform that can help computer forensic investigators to perform searches in an effective way. Some of the modern day SOC solutions offer additional tools for reassembly network forensics and session analysis. A properly implemented SOC is very instrumental in achieving a shorter recovery time from attacks.

SOC Topology

Along with the aggregation of security logs collected from different end points, an SOC will also act as the aggregation point for other kinds of data like, Full Packet Captures, session statistics information, flow data and other traces like audit trails produced by different endpoints and network infrastructure security devices.

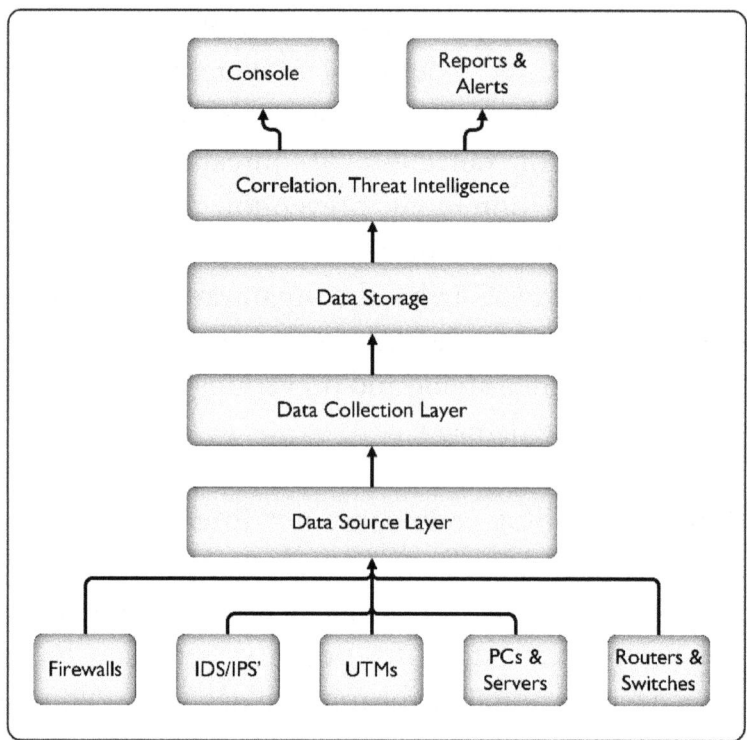

Figure 1 SIM / SIEM Architecture

SOC Reports

SOC solutions offer different kinds of reports targeting different classes of consumers. For example, an executive summary report will only have a brief coverage of the incident plus damage in dollars this incident would have caused to the organizations, or the possible damage it may create if it goes unattended. Such a report is aimed to help the "C" Level team (CSO, CEO, CISO, CTO) to make a quick decision on how to respond to such an event and also to prevent the chances of such an event in future.

The audit and compliance reports offered by Security Monitoring Solutions helps organizations in positioning them in a better way close to the requirements of common regulatory compliance standards. For example, the PCI-DSS Solution pack offered by NETIQ Sentinel offers provision to check all the possible security controls mentioned in PCI-DSS Version-3 standards.

The targeted audience for a technical report produced by SIEM that covers all the aspects of an attack are security analysts and other technical operations team members responsible for mitigation of threats. Such reports may even include recommendations for mitigations, which will help the decision makers in the redefinition of existing security controls or creation of new ones.

In-House SOC vs Outsourced SOC

An organization may opt for Managing, Maintaining and Monitoring the SOC from their premises itself. There are several advantages in setting up an In-House SOC. These include and are not limited to the availability of dedicated technical staff who knows the internal infrastructure of the organization in a better way compared to the MSSP professionals with limited knowledge about the Internal Infrastructure, this helps the SOC analyst in correctly judging the security of an incident.

In-House SOC operations can be tailor made as per the business requirement. The efficiency of an operation of an In-House SOC may be better than MSSP's offering. The major downside of an In-House/Co-operate SOC is the huge initial and periodic investment needed on the Hardware Gear, Storage, Place and Power. There is no way to guarantee the Return of Investment(ROI) in case of an In- House SOC. This makes it extremely difficult to find a compliant security analyst, the chances of building a SOC with the existing resources may be highly risky due to the fact that even seasoned security analyst sometimes miss critical incidents. The chances of collusion between the security analyst and the attacker is increased in the case of an In-House SOC. Not every organization needs its own SOC. The decision to have In-House own SOC should be made with careful analysis.

The factors to consider include:

1. Size/Type of the organization.
2. Number of Incidents reported/noticed in the past.
3. IT budget of the organization.
4. Business/Compliance Requirements

Ready availability of competent SOC analysts having proper expertise in handling different security monitoring solutions and other analysis tools makes an outsourced SOC an attractive option for organizations. Outsourced SOC's are highly scalable and flexible when compared to the In- House offering. Strict SLAs provides finer control of operation and moreover the chances of collusion between the analyst and attacker is minimal. Unbiased decisions and exposure to multiple sets of customers of same segments makes the MSSP security analyst a better choice. The capital retentions associated with an MSSP is less, improper data handling and the storage of the logs off premises brings in additional staff, who know the internal environment, and limited customization options may sometimes make MSSP a less preferred choice.

Outsourced SOC – Service Level Agreements

Response time for different security needs, should be well defined in the SLA. It can range from few hours to even weeks. The top priority, high severity incident, which demands an initial response time of one hour followed by periodic updates every thirty minutes. SLAs may about the escalation and re-prioritization procedures. For example: The priority to security incident may be escalated and converted to priority one incident by the customer. In some cases, the SOC engineer or customer lowers the priority of the incident after the basic analysis of the incident. The procedures/steps to follow in case of an incident, must be well defined in an SLA. Adherence to change management process in case revision of security controls should be considered in SLA. Missing an incident/improper handling of the incident by SOC professional may result penalty. Penalty sometimes may result in termination of the existing contract. Assurance of no reoccurrence of an event, protection against emerging threats and proper effective utilization of Threat Intelligence Data should also be documented. SLAs are meant for improving the quality of the operation, it can be used as a tool by the customer to ensure proper operation of out sourced SOC. The outsourcing contracts normally will include clauses of eventual termination at the end of the contract. The client needs to define and develop a proper exist strategy to ensure smooth transition. The client will plan for either an in house SOC /move to another MSSP provider towards the end of existing contract. This process of transition and associated steps should also be documented. Formal service level metrics are commonly used for measuring the quality of SOC operations. At the end of the contract, if the client is going for an in-house SOC, the existing MSSP partner needs to arrange a number of knowledge transfer sessions Weekly performance reviews verifies the SOC functions. In case of transitioning to an in-house SOC, the MSSP partner will have to work with the internal CIRT team. In some cases, transition is planned phase by phase. For example: The client will only start with, few Tier-2 engineers and all Tier-1 monitoring functions will be handled by the MSSP partner. Once the management has enough confidence the Tier-1 monitoring will also be taken away from the MSSP partner.

The performance review process will analyze:

A. Response – Make sure that the people who are responding to competent enough to handle the situation.

B. Reports – The ability of the SOC team to create a different kind of complete SOC reports, that business demands should be checked.

C. Alerts – Make sure that you are getting timely alerts from the MSSP partner on new and in-progress security incidents.

D. Threat Analysis- The threat analysis capabilities of the MSSP team can be measured by taking few sample incidents from the past few weeks.

SOC Analyst – Desired Skill Set

A Security Analyst is expected to have good proficiency in handling different operating systems. Linux is the most commonly used operating system flavor in SOC environments. Majority of the SOC Monitoring solution are built in Linux for configuring data connection from different end points, decent understanding of different features of the operating system is needed. Now Operating Systems offers centralized event log collection. Centralized event log collection needs a server and a number of client (subscriber) computers, more details about windows centralized event configuration can be found at (link). A security analyst must have good expertise on network security devices like intrusion detection system, Intrusion prevention system, firewall, UTM, etc. He also needs to be familiar with directory access protocols like LDAP, database management systems, flat file system storage, various scripting languages, regular expressions, computer forensic tools and information security policy writing. Ethics and integrity are unavoidable qualities of a security monitoring professional. Moreover, he needs to have good reading habits, problem solving skills and management capabilities. A security Analyst needs to be an abstract thinker and he should respond well to very frustrating situations. He should be extremely curious about the final details of an incident. He must be aware of all the low-level details while keeping big picture of situation. It is extremely difficult to find competent SOC analysts, it may few months to locate someone competent enough. Internal knowledge transfers sessions external technology and product training helps SOC analyst to gain the required knowledge. Attrition is a very common issue a SOC. To reduce the rate of attrition, the frequent bonuses, other perks, management opportunities and promotions are given. Companies may sponsor family holiday trips and reduce the stress related issues. Job rotation is also done. SOC is a highly process oriented set of practices. The proper execution SOC needs well defined documentation, that covers all the SOC functions. Ad-hock manner of working is not suitable for a SOC. Pre-defined work flows ensures smooth SOC operations.

SOC Roles

Role	Strategic	Incident Response	Day to Day
CSO	Strategic Advice Metrics Gathering		
Security Manager		Metrics Gathering IR over-sight	Metrics Gathering
SOC SME		Issue Triage Investiga-tion	
Security Analyst			Investiga-tions Mon-itoring & Alerting Device con-figuration Manage-ment Vulnerabili-ty Manage-ment

Table 2 SOC Roles

Security Analyst

Security Analyst ensures that all the tools deployed in a SOC environment are running optimally. They the monitor the organizational environment continuously for threats, in fact they are front line of security operations most of the time A security analyst will be first point of contact and the interface between different organizational team responsible for mitigation, when a high risk alert or suspected attack begins to affect the business organizations. They are also responsible for the initial phase of forensic investigation.

SME/ Research Specialist

A Security specialist with vast technical expertise and wide experience will be acting as the SME/Research specialist. He will be called on to assist with security incidents that are complex and escalated by other low Tier teams. He normally acts as a consultant to the SOC manager and CISO. The SOC SME is responsible for all kinds of research including things like integration of existing, SOC solutions with threat intelligence feeds, setting up of Network Security Monitoring solutions like Security Onion, STIX/TAXII support etc. SOC SME may be asked to provide POC's (Proof of Concept) on various technical integration requirements. Internal knowledge transfer, review of different vendor products, Revision of existing SOC controls, developing the SOC management frameworks etc. are also the functions of SME.

SOC Manager

SOC Manager translates the Chief Information Security officer's goals and requirements in to set of actions for the SOC team to execute. There will be several issues which needs executive attention or investment. The SOC manager conveys their issues to the CISO and works close with the management to get the necessary approval on budget. The SOC manager acts as an interface between SOC Engineers and CISO. He oversees day to day security operations of the SOC, ensures availability of the resources (people), tools, processes and measurement methods. Talent acquisition is another major responsibility of SOC manager.

Chief Information Security Officer (CISO)

This champion "C" member acts as the primary interface between Security organization and the business owner. He ensures that SOC resources and activities are aligned to the organization business strategy. He is responsible for translating business requirements into security operations objectives. He is expected to educate business executives about how security can enable business innovations. Budget prioritization is another key responsibility of CISO.

Information Needed by SOC Roles

Role	Information Needed
Analysts	• Log and flow data to provide contextual view of security incidents • Alerts which are prioritized based on severity • Access to threat intelligence (TI) feeds • Access to Session analysis, Network forensics & other tools
SOC SME	• Data on emerging threats • End to end and in-depth information on security incidents as they happen to speedup resolution
SOC SME	• Data on SOC resources (staff) management • Up to date status on open security issues
CISO	• Executive summary information on the high priority security risks and incidents. • Overall risk and security posture of the business

Table 3 Information Needed by SOC Roles

Module 2
SIEM Selection and Deployment

How to Select an SIEM Solution?

An Organization making its first SIEM purchase needs to be well aware of the features offered by SIEM product and also the business requirements. Improper decisions may result in overspending on your SIEM solution. The correctly configured and monitored SIEM solution plays a significant role in identifying security breaches near real time. There are various features and characteristics we need to consider when choosing an SIEM product.

Ease of Deployment

SIEM installation and upgrade should be as smooth as possible. I have personally observed several instances of component upgrade failures in large SIEM deployments, failure of components like event processors/collectors will result in stoppage of data collection for several hours.

Very large MNCs may test the upgrade first in their Lab/QA environment to ensure smooth operations. If the upgrade is successful in the QA environment, then only they will plan for the production set up upgrade. Make sure you verify that the data collection process can be automated. Most of the Modern day SIEM solution offers automatic discovery of data collection endpoints in a production environment. The other factors to consider includes ease of migration of data, support for conversion from standalone SIEM deployments to distributed deployment and availability of the SDK/API or support for custom collectors.

Ease of Data Accessibility

Data should be available both for historical and real time analysis. Sometimes as part of forensic investigations/compliance checks, we may be asked to provide access to the archived data. The time needed for accessing the data should be as minimal as possible. Long term storage of excessive amount of logs may need low compression. Generation of reports that includes historical data demands ready availability of index to perform database queries. The local event database of the SIEM solutions will be used for real time threat analysis. Historic analysis may demand access to the log archive and it is most of the time suitable for an in-depth forensic investigation. SIM solutions offer raw log data storage, which will be useful for forensic analysis.

Provision for Threat Intelligence Integration

Integration of threat intelligence feeds with SIEM improves the response time of detection. The indicators of Compromise information data like IPs,

URLs, File Hashes and Domain Information helps the SIEM user in identifying possible threats without even having correlation rules. The contextual information provided by threat intelligence feeds like history of an IP, Risk scoring provided by the Threat Intelligence Source and TIP- Techniques Tactics and Procedures information helps organization in generation of alerts and post threat investigation. The TIP information provided may be helpful in predicting the nature and behavior of an attack. Proper integration of threat intelligence feeds is useful in defining the response course of action. The threat intelligence data is matched with firewall logs, web proxy logs, net flow information, Other networking device logs and NIDS/ NIPS data. Some SIEM vendors produces their own threat intelligence, however most of them now offers customer the provision to integrate multiple threat intelligence feeds in to the SIEM.

In some cases, the SIEM vendor may have their own Threat Intelligence Platform(TIP) that can consume, threat intelligence feeds from both community and commercial providers. The other option is integrating a third-party TIP with the existing SIEM. Threat intelligence is also helpful in validation of correlation rules and relevancy check of a correlation output. Information provided by threat intelligence feeds can be used in reports and alerts as a context for better coverage of threats.

Tools

Your SIEM solution must have integrated tools for converting operational data to actionable information. This tools helps organizations in retracing the actions of the attacker and provides deep insight in to the intrusion activity. Some of the tools are helpful in reassembly and reconstruction of Network streams to its original form. Regular expression can be created and tested from almost all SIEM solutions. Commonly used tracing, editing, searching and capturing tools in Linux environment are available in SIEM CLI. Tools for conversion of event log format, complex reports generations, troubleshooting and debugging, Connectivity issue between connectors and SIEM, disk usage, data migration, manual archiving, scripting etc. are generally expected functions within SIEM products.

Types of Reports

SIEM needs to have capability to generate executive, technical and compliance audit reports as per the business requirements.

SOC Metrics

Event management efficiency of an SIEM should be measured for total raw events, total number of aggregated and analyzed events, total number of correlated events, number of cases opened and initializing of the cases opened. Depending on how many data end points are monitored the amount of raw log data received varies. Additionally, the different types of data collected and the use cases may be considered for measurement of efficiency. The speed of event recognition, event escalation and event resolution is used to calculate the overall response metrics of a SOC.

Further classifications like Per hour / day / week / month, Per security Analyst, Per hour of day/ Per day of week, Case category, Security and number of incidents is also counted in some cases. Effective and efficient service in SOC needs through measurement of people, process and technologies related to security monitoring. Gathered metrics should provide enough information on how well the SOC is operating. The security metrics provides more insight on

- a) Security incidents Trend, is it going up or down?
- b) What is average response time of security operation team on different incidents?
- c) Number of false positions reported
- d) How effective is SOC?
- e) Comparative data on SOC performance with previous month/ quarter/ year information

f)   SOC Head count to incident ratio

How to Select SIEM

Selecting a proper SIEM is not an easy task. Before going ahead with the SIEM selection there must be a log review process in place. Log review process needs a corporate logging policy with the details like the review frequency, log retention period, application requirements and compliance requirements. It is important to enable logging on all needed end points. Proper time stamping ensures correct correlation outputs. The collected logs should be stored in a secure way. The log review process identifies abnormal events that need further investigation. To have this first we need to have an idea about the normal event. Organization normally uses a baseline of the events for this detection. Baseline is created with the reference of already captured events. The baseline enlists different kinds of events and categorizes the events which needs investigations.

The enterprise log management policy needs to have specifications about:

1)   What all relevant logs needs to be captured?
2)   What kinds of events constitute a threat?
3)   Response – time for specific kinds of

threat

4) Response – actions that should be taken.
5) How long the events should be retained?
6) Document when the event occurred and response – action taken.
7) Document follow up actions associated with the event.
8) Document this scope of coverage like which assets needs to be included, which assets are internal etc.
9) Document the record of authority(ROA) that covers the log storage location and the retention period of each class of logs.
10) Create an audit trail that covers the follow up of the list of "Events of Interest" and associated actions.
11) Define and document service level agreements.
12) Define and document standard operating procedures.

There are several players offering log management solutions like ArcSight (logger), Loglogic, Sentinel log manager, Splunk etc. Most of these vendors supports both centralized and distributed log collection. The capability of log management solution to pull logs from different end points like databases, Windows, servers should be checked. A majority of end points can forward logs to the log management solution (via Syslog). Syslog by default works with UDP and does not guarantee the delivery of data. However, syslog can be configured to the work over TCP. It is a common practice to secure the communication channel between the log manager / collector and the end-point to avoid confidentiality attacks against sensitive data. The conventional log management solution requires a lot of manual effort for the log review. SIEM addresses this issue with the help of correlation engine. The default "content" offered by SIEM solution is not adequate enough for threat detection in a production environment. Organization define Events of Internet (EOI) and then use correlation rules to generate alerts to overcome this limitation.

Mosaic security offers a comprehensive SIEM vendor comparison tool which helps you to list your requirements and then generate a short-list of vendors. It compares leading vendor products and then creates personalized list of vendors based on your input. The tool is available at Mosaic security research.com/ SIEM- vendor- shortlist- tool. DCIG SIEM appliance offers comparison of nine leading SIEM products. It is available at DCIG.COM/ guides/ 2014-15-SIEM – appliance- buyers- guide. "Evaluation Criteria for security information and event management document" and "SIEM selection tool" created by ANTON CHUVAKIN of Gartner is another wonderful resource that helps customer to select a proper SIEM solution for the environment. Gartner

Magic quadrant for SIEM provides a qualitative analysis of several security analytics products. Gartner usually rates vendors upon two criteria:

1) Completeness of vision
2) Ability to Execute

Gartner places each vendor in one of the four quadrants:

1) Leaders – With highest score on both criteria
2) Challenges – With more score on ability to execute than completeness of vision
3) Visionaries – With lower ability to execute and higher completeness of vision
4) Niche players – With lower ability to execute and completeness of vision

SOC Functional Modules

The five distinct functional modules of an SIEM are:

1) Event Generators
2) Event Collectors
3) Message Database
4) Analysis Engine
5) Reaction Management Software

These modules are normally built as autonomous part

then combined in a logical way to achieve continuous monitoring and threat response.

Event Generators

All monitored systems act as event generators in SOC. These includes firewalls, IPS/IDS, network equipment's OS's, application, vulnerability assessment and risk assessment tools. Events generators can be broadly classified into two categories, event based generators and status based data generators. Event based data generators or sensors produce events based on specific operation performed on the OS application or over the network. A traffic event generated by an IDS/IPS due to the triggering of an existing rule is a typical example of this. Status based data generators (pollers) produce event data as a reaction to an external process. For example, a ping reply message is created upon the receiving of a ping request. Another good example is an SNMP query probe created by an SNMP manager that generates as output on the probed device which will then be passed back to the enquirer.

Network based or host based IDS is the most commonly seen sensor, other content filtering solutions like Firewalls, Routers, as configured with security controls like ACL's, Switching with L2, L3 security Access control features, wireless Access points and controllers, AAA solutions, DLP boxes, Proxy's, honeypots/honey nets system Integrity verification, Application acceleration solutions, Server Load balancers, Email Security gateways, VPN gateways, SSL Multiplexers, Packet sniffers/Lessing solutions etc.

Sensors – Expected Qualities

Ideally a sensor should have the below capabilities:

1) Continuous operation and fault tolerance: sensors must be fault tolerant it should be able to service a crash without losing data.

2) Resist subversion: The sensor should protect itself from compromise, it should be able to monitor itself continuously.

3) Anti-evasion: A sensor must have the capability to detect and prevent evasion attempts.

4) Overhead: The amount of overhead on log management or SIEM solution should be minimal as possible.

5) Configuration and Scalability: Sensors should be configurable and it should support dynamic configurations.

Pollers generate an alert when a specific state is detected. This is done with the help of preconfigured policies. Pollers are commonly used for service status detects and data integrity checking. For example, NMS solutions like OPEN NMS offers service monitoring with ICMP/SNMP (A free demo of open NMS is available at demo.opennms.org).

Event Collectors

Event collectors are responsible for gathering information from different sensors. They act as log aggregation points. Different end-points uses different log formats. Collectors translate the different formats of logs to a standard format. Collectors connect to a data source either directly or indirectly to collect events. SIEM provides different sets of collectors, in some cases you may develop your own collector with the help of instructions given by the vendor.

To get a clear understanding of collector working let us take a look at OSSEC. OSSEC is a comprehensive host based open source IDS solution that can be integrated with most SIM/SIEM products. An OSSEC Server acts as central hub for all OSSEC agents. SIEM collector aggregates the logs forwarded by the OSSC server. Additionally, customer may opt for direct log forwarding from each OSSEC agent instead of OSSEC SERVER.

```
<ossec_config>
 ...

 <syslog_output>
  <server>192.168.4.1</server>
 </syslog_output>

 <syslog_output>
  <level>10</level>
  <server>10.1.1.1</server>
 </syslog_output>

 ...
</ossec_config>
```

Table 4 Sample OSSEC Syslog Configuration

The direct connection method from collector to end-point can be either with an agent code residing locally or with the help of a native protocol.

Native Protocol Based Direct Connection

Log data either be pushed from the end-point to the collector after the initial configuration of it or in some cases collector must manually request data from endpoint at a regular interval.

Event protocol

With the help of event protocol the event source

communicates with the collector. Some of these protocols support auto configuration and auto discovery. These are a number of event protocols in use.

Let's see different event protocol options in detail:

a) API Based: In this method, the collector uses an API to communicate with the source.

b) OPSEC API: OPSEC (Open Platform for security) is an open, multivendor security frame work.

Other Technology companies can partner with Checkpoint with their OPSEC API's. Log expert API (LEA) and event Logging API (ELA) are the two reporting and logging API's offered by OPSEC. OPSEC LEA uses procedure calls to retrieve the logs. Basically, OPSEC LEA allows you to export logs to third party servers. It allows real time and historical retrieval of logs from checkpoint devices. OPSEC ELA is used for securely sending information to the Checkpoint SMS (Security Management Server). With OPSEC ELA other applications can log security events in Checkpoint Event Log.

Other technologies companies can partner with checkpoint with their OPSEC (open platform for security) API's. OPSEC is open, multivendor security framework with a lot of partners. These are two reporting and logging API's in OPSEC.

LEA – Log Export API
This can be used for real-time and historical retrieval of logs from checkpoint devices.

ELA – Event Logging API
ELA is used for securely sending information to the checkpoint SMS (security Management Server) with ELA other applications can log security event in the checkpoint event log.

Collector to Source Communication Protocol

API based –MSWMI
With the MSWMI SIEM's can collect the Microsoft windows events and data in an agentless way. Windows Management Instructions (WMI) scripts or applications automates administrative tasks in the Windows environment. In fact, MS WMI is based on WBEM (Web based Enterprises management) an industry standard to develop technology for accessing management information in an enterprise environment.

Representation of systems, applications, network, devices and other managed components in WMI is done with the DMTF's (Distributed Management

Task Force) Common Information Model (CIM), remote management connections in WMI uses DCOM. The use of WMI API for log collection needs firewall configurations accept incoming external communication on port 135 and dynamic ports needed by DCOM. There is no polling interval in MS windows security Event Log Protocol (that use WMI) based log collection. This is because of the fact that SIEM's receives event notifications from OS to identify when the events are available. The maximum EPS supported by this method is limited to 50.

Microsoft Security Event Log Over MSRPC Protocol

Microsoft security Event Log over MSRPC can collect only standard windows events. MSRPC does not support retrieval of non-standard windows logs MSRPC can support up to 100 events per second per host so it is suitable for medium sized windows servers. High event rate systems should use dedicated agents to collect and forward logs. MSRPC uses NTLM v2 Session security, so it is best suited in environments where event payload security is needed.

WinRM

Modern day windows OS' has the ability to collect copies of events from multiple remote components and store them locally. You can specify types of events to collect in the event subscription. Forwarding and collecting computers are needed for this. This is achieved with Windows Remote Management Service (WinRM) and Windows Event Collector (Wecsvc). We need to enable both WinRM and Wecsvc services on all collecting and forwarding computers. There are two different methods you can use for centralized windows event log collection using WinRM.

i. **Collector Initiated Event Forwarding /PULL method**

In this method the collector server contacts event sources at regular intervals to determine whether they have logs to transmit. Scalability issues associated with this method limits the use of it in large enterprises environments.

ii. **Source Initiated Subscription**

The remote event log sources forward the logs to a collector server in this method, either HTTP or HTTPS can be used for this forwarding. This is a highly scalable and well suitable model for large enterprise environments. There is no need to specify all the event source computers on an event collection like in collector initiated subscription. Additional configuration steps are needed if the collector computer and all event source computers are in different domain.

More details about this can be found at: https://msdn.microsoft.com/en-us/library/windows/desktop/bb870973(v=vs.85).aspx

SDEE

International Computer Security Association(ICSA) has a new model called SDEE (Security Device Event Exchange) for communication of event generated by security devices. SDEE is highly flexible and allows vendors to extend the standard. Cisco Intrusion Detection Event Exchange (CIDEE) specifics the extensions to SDEE. CIDEE is used in Cisco IPS product.

There are two methods for retrieving events using SDEE:

1) An Event Query
2) Event Subscription

Both of these methods uses SSL to query the SDEE server.

Challenges or Risks in Building a SOC

Right from finding the proper set of people to work in SOC to resolving high-end technical issues, there exist numerous risks in the process of building an SOC.

Below are the major types of risks:

1) Humans
2) Processes and Procedures
3) Legacy and Technology
4) Noise
5) Technical

Humans

It is extremely difficult to find proper set of people with right skills to work in SOC environment. SOC works 24/7 in 365 days. So, the analyst needs to have willingness to work in shifts. In case of geographically distributed SOC environments, language is a concern. The SOC manager has a real challenge in managing the resource/availability of 24/7. Other issue is not all people can apply/avail leaves at a time. SOC has to remain open and operational even during yearly company shut down period. Bonuses and other benefits are commonly used methods for keeping the employees motivated. Periodic technical trainings are also provided to make the security analyst competent with the complex work requirements.

Processes and Procedures

Organizations needs to have well defined and documented processes and procedures to ensure smooth operation of SOC. Companies may develop their own SOC management frameworks for this. Monitoring tools may need integration with the requesting system and ticketing system. It is important to clearly mention the procedure of escalation to follow in case of an incident. Optimization of the processes and procedures will happen overtime with the knowledge learned from the previous incidents.

Legacy and Technologies

While picking the SOC solutions, organizations may look for some legacy on the vendor side. Availability of the configuration guides and other aids, the end of support date and end of life dates needs to be noted. Similarly, companies may also do a valuation of the technologies used in vendor products. This includes, things like the indexing and normalization mechanism in use, online and offline storage methods, searching mechanism used, frontend initialization console, types of reports it can generate, effectiveness of correlation engine etc. Some vendors offer a good collection of default correlation tools and built in dashboards. Almost all vendors support customized dashboards. Rather than going for a solution imposed by a marketing and sales team, one needs to properly analyze different verticals of solutions before making the final call.

Noise

The major sources of noise in SOC are; frequent vulnerability scans, Spam solution alerts, Honeypot activity alerts, ACL/Security logging alerts, IDS/ IPS alerts and Antivirus, Anti spyware and Malware scan related alerts. However, it is extremely important to collect and analyze all relevant security related events before categorizing them as noise. The noise reduction techniques should not be a cause for missing critical events. Sometimes the integration of threat intelligence feeds (Block listed IT reputed list) and the collection of flow data (Net flow, J flow, S flow) may result in noise.

Technical

The throughput of a SOC solution is normally binded to the events/second. Having a low EPS will result in random early drops of the events. You need to note down that random dropping is not priority driven, meaning you may miss even critical events due to this. Maintaining a secure channel between the endpoint and the collector is not always achievable. The additional efforts needed to create custom correlation tools in the absence of built in tools is huge. Careful planning and continuous monitoring helps organizations to resolve these sorts of issues.

Module 3
Managed Security Services SLA

MSSP Service Level Agreement

There should be well written several level agreements between clients and MSSP for network capacity, availability requirements, contingency planning in case of failure, network outage alerts, restoration, escalation and reporting time.

Responsibility of each party for implementing, operating and maintaining security control or mechanisms that must be applied to existing network services should also be documented. Separate legal policy statements for information classification, information retention, evidence admissibility, testification and prosecution procedures should also be there. SLA normally act as a measurable tool for review and performance of an MSSP contract. Improved operational visibility can be guaranteed with a meaningful SLA with proper object criteria's. MSSP generally offers standard service level agreements. If the customer has specific service level agreement to demand, MSSP may go on a negotiation with the customer to make the demanded SLA fit with their general standards.

It is a very usual practice that the customer may demand an enhanced level of service due to the nature of their business. Sometimes an external consultant will be called in by the client to measure the adherence to SLA and also for proposing revisions to the existing SLA. MSSP should take necessary steps to compartmentalize each of its service clients from all other service clients. Other than the basic performance and availability requirement an SLA should also consider common compliance requirements. KPI's (Key Performance Indicators) acts as observable parameters for the measurement of service processes. Penalties for non-compliance and rewards for exceeding expectations are also part of SLA document. Though SLA can be considered as a process description document it constitutes both legal and financial instruments. Careful planning and proper review should be there while defining an SLA to avoid common ambiguities and misunderstandings.

Assessing an SLA

It is extremely important to analyze the SLA for both customer and MSS provider to ensure:

1) That the SLA provides value to the customer.
2) SLA provides a good margin to the service provider with minimal risk.

The terms in SLA should be defined in a way so a customer can correlate and understand its value with their business model. The operational risk associated with each of the agreed terms must be estimated by the service provider. The impact of a failure to meet an

SLA on both the customer's and the service provider's business should be assessed. The service provider must have a framework or a mechanism which will help a client to measure the progress and current status of an SOC operation. Statistical information in the form of reports or other documentation should be provided to the customer in a pre-agreed interval. Cost effectiveness is another factor to be considered before going ahead with a very strict SLA. An SLA should not have any implicit functions that are undefined and result in ambiguity.

Managed Security Services SLA Sample

Listed below is an example of an SLA between MSSP and a customer. The information given below is meant only for the general understanding for a security practitioner and is not a readymade SLA sample to be used in a production environment.

Managed SIEM Appliance Incident Notifications					
	Type of Incident				
Security Incident	Highly Critical	Critical	High	Medium	Low
Response Time	30 Minutes	45 Minutes	60 Minutes	120 Minutes	4-48 Hours
Commit-ment	30 Minutes	45 Minutes	60 Minutes	120 Minutes	4-48 Hours

Table 5 Managed SIEM Appliance Incident Notifications

Managed Log Monitoring Incident Notifications				
	Type of Incident			
Incident Notification Time Commitment	No logging activity	Unavailability of log sources / Connectivity Issues	Unusual logging rate	Corrupted logging / compliance violations
	30 Minutes	30 Minutes	30 Minutes	30 Minutes

Table 6 Managed Log Monitoring Incident Notifications

Standard changes related to Managed Device/service					
	Type of Device				
	Managed UTM	Managed FW, IDS/ IPS, NAC, WAF	Managed Vulnerability Scanning	Managed Log Monitoring	Managed SIEM Appliance
Implementation Time		Within XX hours after getting the request with client manager approval	Within XX hours after getting the request with client manager approval	Within XX hours after getting the request with client manager approval	Within XX hours after getting the request with client manager app

Table 7 Standard changes related to Managed Device/service

Managed Device/service Outage Notifications				
Notification Time Commitment	Managed UTM	Managed FW, IDS/IPS, NAC, WAF	Managed Vulnerability Scanning	Managed Log Monitoring
	20 Minutes	45 Minutes	45 Minutes	45 Minutes

Table 8 Managed Device/service Outage Notifications

Other changes related to Managed Device/service					
	Type of Device				
	Managed UTM	Managed FW, IDS/IPS, NAC, WAF	Managed Vulnerability Scanning	Managed Log Monitoring	Managed SIEM Appliance
Implementation Time		Within XX hours after getting the request with client manager approval	Within XX hours after getting the request with client manager approval	Within XX hours after getting the request with client manager approval	Within XX hours after getting the request with client manager app

Table 9 Other changes related to Managed Device/service

Service Uptime assurance of Managed Device/Service					
	Type of Device				
Response Time	Managed UTM	Managed FW, IDS/IPS, NAC, WAF	Managed Vulnerability Scanning	Managed Log Monitoring	Managed SIEM Appliance
	99.99%	99.96%	99.99%	99.80%	99.99%

Table 10 Service Uptime assurance of Managed Device/Service

Managed device replacement notification					
	Type of Device				
Notification Time	Managed UTM	Managed FW, IDS/IPS, NAC, WAF	Managed Vulnerability Scanning	Managed Log Monitoring	Managed SIEM Appliance
	At least 72 hours in advance after the change confirmation	At least 72 hours in advance after the change confirmation	At least 72 hours in advance after the change confirmation	At least 72 hours in advance after the change confirmation	At least 72 hours in advance after the change confirmation

Table 11 Managed device replacement notification

Managed Vulnerability Scanning Incident Notifications				
Incident Notification Time Commitment to client from MSSP	Failure to scan	Highly Critical vulnerability that needs immediate attention	High severity vulnerability that needs attention	Medium to Low Vulnerability that needs to be noted
	30 Minutes	30 Minutes	4 hours	8 Hours – 48 Hours

Table 12 Managed Vulnerability Scanning Incident
Notifications

Access Control Performance Matrix and Assured Deliverables

Sl. No.	Deliverables	Turnaround Time / Frequency
1	Access failure by prioritized logical grouping (e.g. payment processing resources)	Report once in 7/15/30 days based on the agreed model
2	Top access destinations by users/ groups and anomalous access	Report once in 7/15/30 days based on the agreed model

Sl. No.	Deliverables	Turnaround Time / Frequency
3	Access login success and failure (internal); by user, system, by device class, by time (with details)	Report once in 7/15/30 days based on the agreed model
4	Top access failures by source, destination, user, business unit	Report once in 7/15/30 days based on the agreed model
5	Unusual access to prioritized logical grouping (e.g. financial reporting resources)	Within XX minutes of incident declaration by MSSP SOC team
6	Multiple account log-ons from different geographic locations	Within XX minutes of incident declaration by MSSP SOC team
7	Suspicious access attempts or failure followed by success from same source	Within XX minutes of incident declaration by MSSP SOC team
8	Privileged user access by access failure, by critical resource, by method, by different location/same time	Report once in 7/15/30 days based on agreed model. In case of real time detection of such suspicious event Client management will be informed within XX minutes of incident declaration by MSSP SOC team
9	Top privileged user access follow by configuration changes	Within XX minutes of incident declaration by MSSP SOC team

Sl. No.	Deliverables	Turnaround Time / Frequency
10	Administrative changes to directory service user and group objects; by admin, by user, by group, by resource Criticality	Within XX minutes of incident declaration by MSSP SOC team
11	Use of trusted and service accounts, by volume, by time of day, by domain	Report once in 7/15/30 days based on the agreed model
12	User activations, privilege change and terminations by device class	Report once in 7/15/30 days based on agreed model. In case of real time detection of such suspicious event Client management will be informed within XX minutes of incident declaration by MSSP SOC team
13	Remote access login success and failure (VPN, other); by user, by device class, by time with details	Within XX minutes of incident declaration by MSSP SOC team
14	Unusual service account, terminated account use, login success and failures	Report once in 7/15/30 days based on agreed model. In case of real time detection of such suspicious event Client management will be informed within XX minutes of incident declaration by MSSP SOC team

Table 13 Access Control Performance Matrix and Assured Deliverables

Boundary Defenses Performance Matrix and Assured Deliverables

Sl. No.	Deliverables	Turnaround Time/frequency
1	Top access failures by source and destinations	Report once in 7/15/30 days based on the agreed model
2	Top inbound connections to internal sources by system, user, bandwidth and time	Report once in 7/15/30 days based on the agreed model
3	Top outbound connections to external sources by system, user, bandwidth and time	Report once in 7/15/30 days based on the agreed model
4	Top outbound DMZ connections to external sources by system, user, bandwidth and time	Report once in 7/15/30 days based on the agreed model
5	Top perimeter attacks by category	Report once in 7/15/30 days based on the agreed model
6	Top dropped traffic from DMZ, FW	Report once in 7/15/30 days based on the agreed model

Sl. No.	Deliverables	Turnaround Time/frequency
7	Top blocked internal sources by port, by destinations	Report once in 7/15/30 days based on the agreed model
8	Top blocked outbound connections by port, by destination	Report once in 7/15/30 days based on the agreed model
9	Unusual DNS access and requests	Report once in 7/15/30 days based on agreed model. In case of real time detection of such suspicious event Client management will be informed within XX minutes of incident declaration by MSSP SOC team
10	Changes to active and standby configurations by perimeter device class	Report once in 7/15/30 days based on agreed model. In case of real time detection of such suspicious event Client management will be informed within XX minutes of incident declaration by MSSP SOC team
11	Top unusual peak bandwidth utilization sources and destination	Report once in 7/15/30 days based on the agreed model
12	Top bandwidth by protocol, by connection, by source, by destination	Report once in 7/15/30 days based on the agreed model

Sl. No.	Deliverables	Turnaround Time/frequency
13	Configuration changes FW, VPN, WAP, Domain	Report once in 7/15/30 days based on the agreed model
14	Failure FW, VPN, WAP, Domain	Report once in 7/15/30 days based on agreed model. In case of real time detection of such suspicious event Client management will be informed within XX minutes of incident declaration by MSSP SOC team
15	Multiple login failures by FW, VPN, Domain	Report once in 7/15/30 days based on agreed model. In case of real time detection of such suspicious event Client management will be informed within XX minutes of incident declaration by MSSP SOC team
16	Excessive VM movement by VM, by guest host	Report once in 7/15/30 days based on agreed model. In case of real time detection of such suspicious event Client management will be informed within XX minutes of incident declaration by MSSP SOC team
17	Noncompliance VM movement by VM, by guest host	Report once in 7/15/30 days based on agreed model. In case of real time detection of such suspicious event Client management will be informed within XX minutes of incident declaration by MSSP SOC team

Sl. No.	Deliverables	Turnaround Time/frequency
18	Wireless network access by location, by user, by failed attempts	Report once in 7/15/30 days based on the agreed model

Table 14 Boundary Defenses Performance Matrix and Assured Deliverables

Network and System Resource Integrity Performance Matrix and Assured Deliverables

Sl. No.	Deliverables	Turnaround Time/frequency
1	Installation of unauthorized software:	Report once in 7/15/30 days based on agreed model. In case of real time detection of such suspicious event Client management will be informed within XX minutes of incident declaration by MSSP SOC team
2	Configuration changes outside approved changes (maintaining separate change reference data)	Report once in 7/15/30 days based on agreed model. In case of real time detection of such suspicious event Client management will be informed within XX minutes of incident declaration by MSSP SOC team

Sl. No.	Deliverables	Turnaround Time/frequency
3	Top business critical devices with critical resource utilization (memory, processor, storage, fan)	Report once in 7/15/30 days based on the agreed model
4	Top device / system restarts	Report once in 7/15/30 days based on agreed model. In case of real time detection of such suspicious event Client management will be informed within XX minutes of incident declaration by MSSP SOC team
5	Top process start and failure (filtered)	Report once in 7/15/30 days based on the agreed model
6	Object access denied	Report once in 7/15/30 days based on agreed model. In case of real time detection of such suspicious event Client management will be informed within XX minutes of incident declaration by MSSP SOC team
7	DNS configuration changes	Report once in 7/15/30 days based on agreed model. In case of real time detection of such suspicious event Client management will be informed within XX minutes of incident declaration by MSSP SOC team

Sl. No.	Deliverables	Turnaround Time/frequency
8	DNS faults	Report once in 7/15/30 days based on agreed model. In case of real time detection of such suspicious event Client management will be informed within XX minutes of incident declaration by MSSP SOC team
9	Account changes by critical resource	Report once in 7/15/30 days based on agreed model. In case of real time detection of such suspicious event Client management will be informed within XX minutes of incident declaration by MSSP SOC team
10	Excessive VM movement by VM, by guest host	Report once in 7/15/30 days based on agreed model. In case of real time detection of such suspicious event Client management will be informed within XX minutes of incident declaration by MSSP SOC team
11	Top critical system/ device changes per user, per device class, per IT services	Report once in 7/15/30 days based on the agreed model
12	Unauthorized changes, by criticality, as percentage and trend	Report once in 7/15/30 days based on the agreed model

Sl. No.	Deliverables	Turnaround Time/frequency
13	Changes to configurations by device class, by user, by criticality	Report once in 7/15/30 days based on the agreed model
14	Systems outside configuration standards; by criticality, class, business unit, ratio and trend	Report once in 7/15/30 days based on the agreed model
15	Percent of systems without approved patches	Report once in 7/15/30 days based on the agreed model
16	Top attacks by exploited vulnerable systems	Report once in 7/15/30 days based on the agreed model
17	Top inbound and outbound connections by system, user, bandwidth and time Unusual scanner / probe activities	Report once in 7/15/30 days based on the agreed model
18	Nonstandard port activity	Report once in 7/15/30 days based on agreed model. In case of real time detection of such suspicious event Client management will be informed within XX minutes of incident declaration by MSSP SOC team

Sl. No.	Deliverables	Turnaround Time/frequency
19	Actual and suspected systems with Peer:2:Peer software or communications	Report once in 7/15/30 days based on agreed model. In case of real time detection of such suspicious event Client management will be informed within XX minutes of incident declaration by MSSP SOC team
20	Top system issue/ incident by incident category	Report once in 7/15/30 days based on the agreed model
21	Noncompliance VM movement by VM, by guest host	Report once in 7/15/30 days based on agreed model. In case of real time detection of such suspicious event Client management will be informed within XX minutes of incident declaration by MSSP SOC team
22	High resource utilization by VM guest host, by resource types	Report once in 7/15/30 days based on agreed model. In case of real time detection of such suspicious event Client management will be informed within XX minutes of incident declaration by MSSP SOC team

Sl. No.	Deliverables	Turnaround Time/frequency
23	Devices with unauthorized or anomalous communications (SMTP, etc.)	Report once in 7/15/30 days based on agreed model. In case of real time detection of such suspicious event Client management will be informed within XX minutes of incident declaration by MSSP SOC team
24	Vulnerability to incident ratio and open/closed vulnerability trends	Report once in 7/15/30 days based on the agreed model
25	Attacks against vulnerable systems classified by criticality	Report once in 7/15/30 days based on the agreed model
26	Device/device group availability percentage	Report once in 7/15/30 days based on the agreed model
27	Failed backup services (or other similar services) by system, by time, by business unit/service	Report once in 7/15/30 days based on agreed model. In case of real time detection of such suspicious event Client management will be informed within XX minutes of incident declaration by MSSP SOC team

Table 15 Network and System Resource Integrity Performance Matrix and Assured Deliverables

Host Defenses Performance Matrix and Assured Deliverables

Sl. No.	Deliverables	Turnaround Time/ Frequency
1	IPS/IDS events classified as incidents by network, by service	Report once in 7/15/30 days based on the agreed model
2	Top incidents by attack type, by source, by destination	Report once in 7/15/30 days based on the agreed model
3	Top attack sources and destinations by volume or destination criticality	Report once in 7/15/30 days based on the agreed model
4	Attacks identified and resolved	Report once in 7/15/30 days based on the agreed model
5	Top traffic by source by application, by source type, by business unit	Report once in 7/15/30 days based on the agreed model
6	Unauthorized and suspicious network traffic by source, by destination, by type	Report once in 7/15/30 days based on the agreed model

Sl. No.	Deliverables	Turnaround Time/ Frequency
7	H Suspicious be-haviour by source, by destination, by type	Report once in 7/15/30 days based on the agreed model
8	Suspicious communications by source, by destination, by type	Report once in 7/15/30 days based on the agreed model
9	Attack investigation open and close ratio and trends	Report once in 7/15/30 days based on agreed model. In case of real time detection of such suspicious event Client management will be informed within XX minutes of incident declaration by MSSP SOC team
10	Wireless IDS alerts	Report once in 7/15/30 days based on agreed model. In case of real time detection of such suspicious event Client management will be informed within XX minutes of incident declaration by MSSP SOC team

Table 16 Host Defenses Performance Matrix and Assured Deliverables

Malware Control Performance Matrix and Assured Deliverables

Sl. No	Deliverables	Turnaround Time/Frequency
1	Top reported malware threats	Report once in 7/15/30 days based on the agreed model
2	Anti-virus trends; prevented, detected, remediated	Report once in 7/15/30 days based on the agreed model
3	Spam trends; identified and removed	Report once in 7/15/30 days based on the agreed model
4	Top malware attacked sources, and by prior vulnerability issues	Report once in 7/15/30 days based on the agreed model
5	Top unusual traffic to and from sources	Report once in 7/15/30 days based on the agreed model
6	Top source and destinations of malicious connections	Report once in 7/15/30 days based on the agreed model
7	Top systems with multiple infections / top systems re-infected	Report once in 7/15/30 days based on the agreed model
8	Top systems with suspicious malware activity	Report once in 7/15/30 days based on the agreed model

Sl. No	Deliverables	Turnaround Time/Frequency
9	Anomalous network activity	Report once in 7/15/30 days based on agreed model. In case of real time detection of such suspicious event Client management will be informed within XX minutes of incident declaration by MSSP SOC team
10	Atypical email or web communications	Report once in 7/15/30 days based on agreed model. In case of real time detection of such suspicious event Client management will be informed within XX minutes of incident declaration by MSSP SOC team
11	Atypical port/application use	Report once in 7/15/30 days based on agreed model. In case of real time detection of such suspicious event Client management will be informed within XX minutes of incident declaration by MSSP SOC team
12	Anti-virus stop, start, update failures	Statistical report once in 7/15/30 days as agreed and notification of update failures and signature parsing issues within 30 minutes of incident declaration by MSSP SOC team.

Table 17 Malware Control Performance Matrix and Assured Deliverables

Module 4
Network Security Monitoring

Network Security Monitoring

Network Security Monitoring provides meaningful data for intrusion analysis in the shortest amount of time. NSM is the comprehensive collection of data to ease the process of analysis to detect and respond into intrusions. Todd Heberlein developed network security monitoring in 1998, it was a kind of intrusion detection system that used live or offline network traffic as its input. In 1993 Air force Computer Emergency Responds Team (AFCERT) with the help of Heberlein developed Automated Security Insuring Measurement System(ASIMS). Most of the modern-day organizations build their own Computer Incident Respond Team (CIRT).

CIRT team members use NSM:

i. To collect and aggregate all network derived data.
ii. To analyze the captured network data to identify intrusions or intrusion attempts.
iii. To define the response strategy, in case of an attack.
iv. To perform forensic analysis and risk or damage analysis.

NSM is not responsible for directly preventing intrusions, but it will help the organization to identify the attempts and prevent the objectives of adversaries. Data provided by the NSM is very useful in predicting the objectives of an attacker. It is in fact quite difficult to detect data exfiltration attempts by using conventional security solutions.

Network Security Monitoring and Continuous Security Monitoring are not the same thing. NSM focuses on adversaries and CSM is based on vulnerabilities. Continuous Security Monitoring alone cannot give you sufficient protection from all threats. The good part is NSM helps organizations to contain the activities of adversaries   before they complete their mission.

Security platforms like intrusion Prevention System, Content Filtering Solution, Antivirus etc. focuses on blocking or denying the attack from happening. NSM can be used for providing better visibility of different phases of an attack.

NSM Deployment

The CIRT team with the help of the network infrastructure management engineers configures layer 2 switches to export copies of the traffic to the NSM server. The NSM server needs to have all the software needed for traffic analysis. It may not be practically possible to collect all the network traffic from all available switches. Moreover, doing so   may result in   duplicate collection of data at NSM server so it is important to properly identify the switches on which the exporting feature has to be enabled. Some organizations may opt for dedicated hardware based network taps instead of configuring the switches for exporting the data. There are number of companies offering different hardware tapping solutions to achieve this.

SPAN

Switch Port Analyzer (SPAN) can be used for exporting the network traffic from a switch if both NSM mirrored port is on the same switch.

Below example shows how to set up a SPAN session for monitoring source port traffic to a destination port in a Cisco switch.

```
Switch(config)# no monitor session 1
Switch(config)# monitor session 1 source interface fastEthernet0/1
Switch(config)# monitor session 1 destination interface fastEthernet0/10 encapsulation dot1q
Switch(config)# end
```

RSPAN (Remote Switch Port Analyzer)

RSPAN is used in scenarios where the NSM is located at a different switch port than the monitoring switch port.

Below example shows how to configure a RSPAN session to monitor multiple source interfaces, and configure the destination RSPAN VLAN and the reflector-port in source and destination Cisco switches.

Source Switch

Switch(config)# monitor session 1 source interface fastEthernet0/10 tx
Switch(config)# monitor session 1 source interface fastEthernet0/2 rx
Switch(config)# monitor session 1 source interface fastEthernet0/3 rx
Switch(config)# monitor session 1 source interface port-channel 102 rx
Switch(config)# monitor session 1 destination remote vlan 901 reflector-port fastEthernet0/1
Switch(config)# end

Destination Switch

Switch(config)# monitor session 1 source remote vlan 901
Switch(config)# monitor session 1 destination interface fastEthernet0/5
Switch(config)# end

NSM Limitations

Network security Monitoring is a difficult to implement task in the case of enterprise wireless networks. Wireless end hosts communicate with each other in an encrypted way. This makes NSM ineffective however, this is applicable only in the case of node to node wireless communication. If a wireless host accesses the internet or any other corporate website this traffic has to traverse through the enterprise network.

If mobile hosts are using cellular networks within enterprise environment you may need to get necessary legal approval before tapping the data.

NSM Data Types

Network Security Monitoring deals with or captures different kinds of data. These include:

- Full Content Data
- Extracted Content Data
- Transaction Data
- Session Data
- Statistical Data
- Meta Data
- Alert Data

Full Content Data Analysis

Full content data is the exact copy of a network traffic.

The security analyst can perform two major types of analysis with this kind of data.

Full Content Data Summary Analysis

In this type of analysis security analyst looks into summary of the captured data. This is generally done by looking into the header details of the packets. The below example shows the use of Tcpdump tool for summary data analysis.

Full Content Data – Individual Packet Analysis

In this security analyst picks some sample packets out of the whole captured data and then performs a full inspection of it. Hexadecimal and ASCII representation of the packets will be used for analysis, from L2 to L7 (payload) command line tools like "tcpdump" or GUI tools like "Wireshark" can be used for this kind of analysis.

The below example shows the use of Tcpdump tool

```
# tcpdump -nnvvXSs 1514 -c 2
tcpdump: data link type PKTAP
tcpdump: listening on pktap, link-type PKTAP (Packet Tap),
capture size 1514 bytes
17:58:39.128544 IP (tos 0x0, ttl 64, id 48715, offset 0, flags
[DF], proto TCP (6), length 76)
    192.168.1.4.63423 > 188.172.192.5.5938: Flags [P.],
cksum 0x0b1d (correct), seq 2586084325:2586084349,
ack 3333128064, win 4130, options [nop,nop,TS val
262368849 ecr 566659564], length 24
        0x0000:  3c1e 0434 0a13 a099 9b15 943f 0800
4500 <..4.......?..E.
        0x0010:  004c be4b 4000 4006 3e02 c0a8 0104
bcac .L.K@.@.>.......
        0x0020:  c005 f7bf 1732 9a24 83e5 c6ab 7f80 8018
.....2.$........
        0x0030:  1022 0b1d 0000 0101 080a 0fa3 6e51
21c6 ."..........nQ!.
        0x0040:  89ec 1130 1b00 0000 0000 0f00 0000
1200 ...0............
        0x0050: 0000 1b00 0000 1800 0000          ..........
17:58:39.554518 IP (tos 0x0, ttl 116, id 24523, offset 0,
flags [DF], proto TCP (6), length 76)
    188.172.192.5.5938 > 192.168.1.4.63423: Flags [P.],
cksum 0x1ca3 (correct), seq 3333128064:3333128088, ack
2586084349, win 515, options [nop,nop,TS val 566664557
ecr 262368849], length 24
        0x0000:  a099 9b15 943f 3c1e 0434 0a13 0800
4500 .....?<..4....E.
        0x0010:  004c 5fcb 4000 7406 6882 bcac c005 c0a8
.L_.@.t.h.......
        0x0020:  0104 1732 f7bf c6ab 7f80 9a24 83fd 8018
...2.......$....
```

Extracted Content Data Analysis

Extracted content data analysis focuses on high level stream content rather than the MAC, IP and protocol headers. Videos, images, other files etc. exchanged between computers can be analyzed in detail through this method.

Extracted content data analysis sometimes needs reconstructions or reassembly of streams. Xplico is an open source tool which can be used for this reconstruction of session.

Below screenshot shows the reassembly of a mms page using Xplico.

Figure 2 Xplico Interface

Transaction Data Analysis

Transaction data analysis focuses on requests and responses exchanged between endpoints. For example, a legitimate HTTP session will have GET requests followed by a 200 OK or not found response messages. If you are finding HTTP POST without an associated HTTP GET it may be an indication of a data exfiltration attempt using HTTP POST. Network Security Monitoring uses tools like Bro for transaction data analysis.

Session Data Analysis

Session data is the complete end to end communication record between two end hosts. Transaction data is only a subset of session data with details like Source Address, Destination Address, Source Port, Destination port, Session start time, Session end time, amount of bytes or data transferred, protocols used and timestamp.

Open source tools like Bro and Sguil are commonly used for this kind of analysis.

Bro Alerts

```
CaptureLoss::Too_Much_Loss              SSH::Password_Guessing
Conn::Ack_Above_Hole                    SSH::Watched_Country_Login
Conn::Content_Gap                       SSL::Certificate_Expired
Conn::Retransmission_Inconsistency      SSL::Certificate_Expires_Soon
DNS::External_Name                      SSL::Certificate_Not_Valid_Yet
FTP::Bruteforcing                       SSL::Invalid_Server_Cert
FTP::Site_Exec_Success                  Scan::Address_Scan
HTTP::SQL_Injection_Attacker            Scan::Port_Scan
HTTP::SQL_Injection_Victim              Signatures::Count_Signature
Intel::Notice                           Signatures::Multiple_Sig_Responders
PacketFilter::Dropped_Packets           Signatures::Multiple_Signatures
ProtocolDetector::Protocol_Found        Signatures::Sensitive_Signature
ProtocolDetector::Server_Found          Software::Software_Version_Change
SMTP::Blocklist_Blocked_Host            Software::Vulnerable_Version
SMTP::Blocklist_Error_Message           TeamCymruMalwareHashRegistry::Match
SMTP::Suspicious_Origination            Traceroute::Detected
SSH::Interesting_Hostname_Login         Weird::Activity
SSH::Login_By_Password_Guesser
```

Figure 3 Bro Alerts

Sguil Session data analysis output

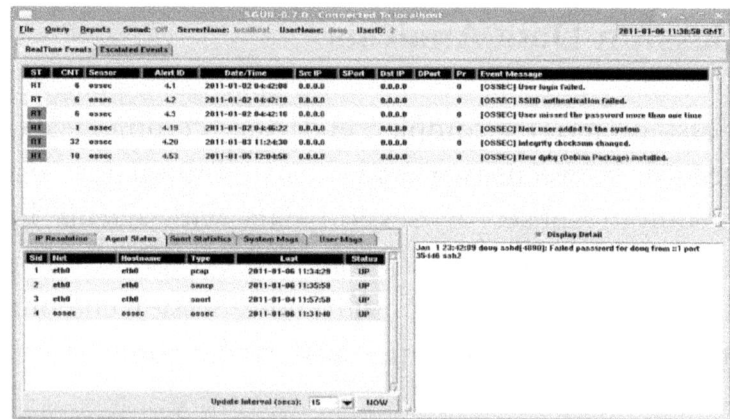

Figure 4 Sguil Session data analysis output

Argus is another nice tool which can be used for session data analysis.

Statistical Data Analysis

As the name implies this kind of analysis focuses on the statistical information like file /data size, start and end time of transfer etc. Wireshark or Capinfos (bundled with Wireshark) can be used for this kind of analysis. Wireshark offers different kinds of statistical data information.

Wireshark endpoint statistics

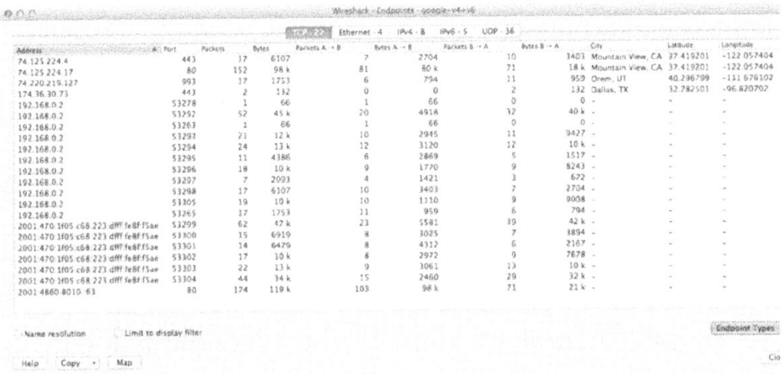

Address	Port	Packets	Bytes	Packets A → B	Bytes A → B	Packets B → A	Bytes B → A	City	Latitude	Longitude
74.125.224.4	443	17	6107	7	2704	10	3403	Mountain View, CA	37.419201	-122.057404
74.125.224.17	80	152	98 k	81	80 k	71	18 k	Mountain View, CA	37.419201	-122.057404
74.220.219.127	993	17	1753	6	794	11	959	Orem, UT	40.296799	-111.676102
174.36.30.73	443	2	132	0	0	2	132	Dallas, TX	32.782501	-96.820702
192.168.0.2	53278	1	66	1	66	0	0	-	-	-
192.168.0.2	53292	52	45 k	20	4918	32	40 k	-	-	-
192.168.0.2	53263	1	66	1	66	0	0	-	-	-
192.168.0.2	53293	21	12 k	10	2945	11	9427	-	-	-
192.168.0.2	53294	24	13 k	12	3120	12	10 k	-	-	-
192.168.0.2	53295	11	4386	6	2869	5	1517	-	-	-
192.168.0.2	53296	18	10 k	9	1770	9	8243	-	-	-
192.168.0.2	53297	7	2093	4	1421	3	672	-	-	-
192.168.0.2	53298	17	6107	10	3403	7	2704	-	-	-
192.168.0.2	53305	19	10 k	10	1110	9	9008	-	-	-
192.168.0.2	53265	17	1753	11	959	6	794	-	-	-
2001:470:1f05:c68:223:dfff:fe8f:f5ae	53299	62	47 k	23	5581	39	42 k	-	-	-
2001:470:1f05:c68:223:dfff:fe8f:f5ae	53300	15	6919	8	3025	7	3894	-	-	-
2001:470:1f05:c68:223:dfff:fe8f:f5ae	53301	14	6479	8	4312	6	2167	-	-	-
2001:470:1f05:c68:223:dfff:fe8f:f5ae	53302	17	10 k	8	2972	9	7678	-	-	-
2001:470:1f05:c68:223:dfff:fe8f:f5ae	53303	22	13 k	9	3061	13	10 k	-	-	-
2001:470:1f05:c68:223:dfff:fe8f:f5ae	53304	44	34 k	15	2460	29	32 k	-	-	-
2001:4860:8010::63	80	174	119 k	103	98 k	71	21 k	-	-	-

Figure 5 Wireshark endpoint statistics

Meta Data Analysis

Data about data is known as metadata. External tools or resources like whois, ip2config, robotex.com etc. are used for meta data analysis. IP reputation lookup and other kind of threat intelligence information is also useful for this analysis.

Alert Data

Intrusion detection systems triggers events when they interpret data traffic. The events generated by security Appliances upon devices of matching condition is called Alert. Snort and Suricata are the two most commonly used open source solution.

Snort and Sguil are used for alert data analysis.

NSM Deployment

Organizations must decide on the type of network traffic they need to monitor before going ahead with NSM.A thorough analysis of network traffic needs to be performed to identify the placement locations of NSM sensors. An NSM server can be either a commercially available appliance or something we build on your own.

There may be multiple monitoring interfaces in an NSM server. It is a fairly good idea to allocate one or more CPU core per monitoring interface. A basic deployment of NSM needs a bare minimum of 8GB RAM. There should be adequate space available for the storage of the network traffic and other NSM data. Normally RAID is used in storage.

NSM Deployment models

NSM Deployment can be either, standalone or Distributed.

Stand-alone NSM

In a standalone NSM deployment a single NSM instance acts as sensor and server. This model is suitable for small and medium based companies. Typically, it is used in scenarios where there is only one segment is being monitored. All the functions of the NSM like monitoring analysis and reporting is performed by one single box.

Distributed NSM

An all in one box approach is not suitable for very large and complicated enterprise network environments. We need to segment the process of collection, analysis and reporting separately to make the NSM scalable for this kind of requirements. Multiple sensors placed at different locations collect and interpret traffic and then forwards the collected data to the NSM server. Distributed models can monitor multiple network segments effectively.

Commonly Used Tools for Building NSM

NSM is a collection of different open source tools for advanced threat analysis. The commonly used tools include and not limited to:

- ⊖ SGUIL
- ⊖ SQERT
- ⊖ BRO
- ⊖ ELSA
- ⊖ Xplico
- ⊖ Argus
- ⊖ SANCP

SGUIL

It uses a number of tools for its different functions. MySQL 4.x/5.x is used as the back-end storage mechanism. The intrusion detection engine uses either SNORT/SURICATA. IDS alert decoding is done with the help of Berniyard or Berniyard-2. TCP IP session recording is with the SANCP. OS fingerprinting tool used is p0f. TCPdump and Wireshark are used for session and packet analysis.

SQERT

SQERT is a simple web application, that is used to query the SGUIL backend database. The visual frontend of the SQERT provides contextual information like Metadata, Grouped Result sets, Time series representations etc.

SQERT instruction image and a demo is available at: http://github.com/int13h/SQERT

BRO

BRO is basically an advanced traffic analyzer, that can analyze all traffic for signs of suspicious activities. BRO provides different sets of log files that carries information about network activity in detail. The application layer details like HTTP URI's, MIME types, DNS responses, SMTP session details etc. are very useful in advanced traffic analysis. BRO by default provides binary extraction from http sessions. The extracted binary files can be further analyzed with the help of external tools. The other functions offered by BRO includes Malware detection, Vulnerable software detection, Brute-Force attack detection and SSL certificate validation. BRO is very customizable and extensible.

The Heart of BRO is an Event Engine that converts packet streams (Network Streams) into a series of higher level events. The events are derived in such a way that it will represent the network activity in a policy neutral way. The policy script interpreter executes, Event handlers and extracts properties from the events.

ELSA

Enterprise Log Search and Archive (ELSA) provides a fully asynchronous web based query interface, that will help the security analyst to search for any arbitrary strings from billions of stored records. The framework used is based on Syslog-NG, the backend storage is with MySQL and full text search functionality is provided by Phinx.

The records can be either logs or alerts. A single instance of ELSA can receive and index more than 30K events per seconds. It supports active directory/LDAP integration for authentication and authorization. For highly scalable requirements distributed architecture with clusters is recommended. ELSA is capable of generating Ad-hock reports/graphs based on arbitrary queries even on very large data sets. ELSA uses Google Visualization for dashboards. Normalization is by default available for CISCO logs, SNORT/ SURICATA, BRO, SNARE etc.

Xplico

Xplico is an advanced network forensic analysis tool, that supports reconstruction of data with the ability to recognize the different protocols with a method called PIPI (Port Independent Protocol Identification). Xplico can extract content like images, files, cookies, videos etc. from web sessions. It is also very useful in email analysis, as it supports reconstruction of IMAP, POP and SMTP protocol data. The other protocol Xplico can reconstructed are VOIP, MSN IRC HTTP and FTP.

Xplico System Architecture

There are Four major components in Xplico system architecture:

1. Dema
2. Xplico
3. Data Manipulators
4. Visualization Systems

Dema (Decoding Manager) is responsible for:

a) Input data handling
b) Manage configurations and History files for the decoder and the manipulators.
c) Launch the decoders and the manipulators
d) Control the execution of decoders and

Manipulators

The Xplico decoder reads the raw data from capture dissector block and then forwards it to the protocol dissector's block. Finally, the dispatcher block handles re-organization of the reconstructed and normalized data or sends it to manipulator as needed.

Argus

Argus is a powerful real time flow monitor, that offers comprehensive data network traffic auditing. Argus reports are suitable for historical and near real-time processing for forensics trends and alarm/alerting. Argus can read packets directly from network interface and classify it into network transactions.

You can find more details about Argus at: http://qosient.com/argus

SANCP

SANCP (Security Analyst Network Connection Profiler) is commonly used for statistical network traffic analysis. SANCP is capable of creating connection logs and record network traffic for the purpose of auditing, historical analysis, and network activity discovery.

Module 5
Event Source Categories and the Recommended Use Cases

Event Source Categories and the Recommended Use Cases

The guidelines provided in this module helps SOC professionals in understanding and responding to security monitoring requirements in a more professional manner. Additionally, the use cases and correlation rules proposed in this module aids in making the security monitoring service more relevant to the threat landscape. The use cases recommended are for the event source category.

The major event source categories considered are -

- Θ Anti-spam
- Θ Anti-virus
- Θ End-point threat protection/Application control/whitelisting solution
- Θ Web/Application server or database
- Θ Data loss prevention /File integrity monitor
- Θ Financial application
- Θ Host based firewall
- Θ Single sign on
- Θ IPS/IDS
- Θ Network based firewall
- Θ Network user behavior analysis
- Θ Operating system
- Θ Storage

- ⊖ VPN
- ⊖ Vulnerability Scanning solution
- ⊖ NAC solution

Anti-Spam

There are several solutions like gateway based filters, client side applications and mail server integrated solutions for anti-spam. The gateway filters are dedicated anti-spam solutions that are often coupled with anti-virus to provide an end to end mail filtering service.

Gateway filters off-load the performance and bandwidth consumption issues of running them on the mail server directly. Mail servers integrated anti-spam solutions run on the server directly processes the spam inline. Client side application that runs on end user's system directly to process spam is not widely-used solutions in a corporate environment. However, the heuristic capabilities of these solutions and lower pricing makes it the perfect choice for a home user.

Anti-Spam Detection and Processing Techniques

Anti-spam solutions use different techniques for the detection and processing of spam. These includes and not limited to:

1. Hashing or checksums
2. Open relay checks
3. RBL check
4. Bayesian filter
5. Heuristic
6. Signatures
7. Black listing and white listing

Hashing or Checksums

Hash values of specific portion of the spam emails is computed and stored in the anti-spam solutions. An email that matches the stored hash will be flagged as spam.

Open Relay Checks

Open relay checks verify whether source mail server permit relays. Mail servers that are configured to relay can be misconfigured by the attacker to limit problem with SPAM black listing. Anti-spam solutions block email from source servers that permits relaying.

RBL check

Malicious Anti-spam solutions may use the real time black lists for blocking spam emails.

Bayesian Filter

Bayesian filters uses user input for calculating the statistical probability an email spam.

Heuristic

The probability of spam is calculated statistically by the combination of a variety of detection mechanism to recognize specific patterns that indicates spam.

Signatures

Specific keywords within a message are checked for the identification of spam.

Black Listing and White Listing

In black listing the anti-spam solution blocks messages from a specific user defined source address, domain or IP. Anti-spam solutions can also be configured to permit messages from user defined white list only.

Anti-Spam Event Categories

As a security analyst one should consider developing and implementing at least the below set of recommended use cases and correlation rules for an anti-spam event source.

Below are the major event source categories to be considered from security perspective.

- ⊖ Email spam
- ⊖ Instant messaging spam
- ⊖ Comment spam
- ⊖ Junk FAX (Out of Scope for Security Analytics)
- ⊖ Internet telephony spam
- ⊖ Unsolicited text messages (Out of Scope for Security Analytics)

Recommended Use Cases and Correlation Rules

Sl. No.	Use Case	Event Type/ Category	Correlation Rule
1	Trigger alert for the EMAIL SPAM originated from inside host.	General Email SPAM	ATYPICAL/ UNUSUAL outbound Email , possible SPAM

Sl. No.	Use Case	Event Type/ Category	Correlation Rule
2	Trigger alert for SPAM in the incoming Email with RBL , IP reputation & MIME header checks.	General Email SPAM	ATYPICAL/UN-USUAL inbound Email, possible SPAM TOP SPAM sources reported
3	Trigger Alarm if Phishing content is found in an email	General Email SPAM	PHISHING con-tent inside email , possible spear phishing attempt/ SPAM
4	Trigger Alarm if SPAM con-tent is found in an IM flow	Instant messag-ing spam	ATYPICAL/ UNUSUAL In-stant messaging communication detected, possible SPAM
5	Trigger Alarm if SPAM content is found in a VOIP flow	Internet Tele-phony SPAM	ATYPICAL/ UNUSUAL In-ternet Telephony communication detected, possible SPAM

Table 18 Recommended Use Cases and Correlation Rules

Antivirus

Anti-malware software helps in the prevention, detection and removal of malicious software. The modern-day antivirus programs are capable of providing protection against malicious browser help objects (BHO), key loggers, backdoors, Trojans, rootkits, worms, adware, spyware, spam, phishing attacks, APT, privacy threats and DDOS attacks.

The common detection method incudes:

- Θ Sand boxing – Behavioral-based detection by allowing the program execution in a sandboxed environment and capturing all its actions.

- Θ Data mining – Data mining and machine learning algorithms classify the behavior of a file (as either malicious or benign) given a series of file features that are extracted from the file itself.

- Θ Signature based detection – Compares the suspected file or pattern with its signature database to detect known threats.

- Θ Heuristics – Compares the suspected files or pattern with the generic signature specific to a Virus Family.

- Θ Behavioral-based – Detection based on the behavioral pattern of the malware.

- Θ Root kit detection - A combination of advanced detection techniques is used for this.

Event Categories

The three major categories of events to be considered from an Antivirus event source for effective security monitoring are –

1. AV Definition / Signature Database Status events – Helps the Security Analyst detect the state of protection and virus and spyware signature definitions updates.
2. Scan - antivirus scan related events.
3. Treatment –events related to the action done to the infected files.

Recommended Use Cases and Correlation Rules

Sl. No.	Use Case	Event Type	Correlation Rule
1	To monitor antivirus software logs to track if detected viruses are cleaned properly.	AV Scan	Failed AV mitigation or cleaning detected, possible persistent virus infection.
2	Identify machines that are not updated to the latest AV definitions.	AV Update	Detect unprotected end points, possible Antivirus disable attempt. Detect Anti-virus stop, start, update failures.
3	Identify machines that are updated to the latest AV definitions.	AV Update	Report of the Current AV protection Posture
4	Identify quarantine action failed events.	AV Scan	Report of Anti-virus trends; prevented, detected, remediated

Sl. No.	Use Case	Event Type	Correlation Rule
5	To monitor access requests to fixed- function end-point devices, such as point-of-sale (POS), medical equipment, Industrial control systems, SCADA, aeronautical system & to prevent unauthorized access attempts.	PoS	Detect unauthorized access attempts to fixed-functions in end points
6	To perform user / Administrator activity monitoring & to ensure compliance.	UAM	Detect unusual user activity
7	Identify events where the user chose to delete an item.	AV-Treatment	Track forced file removal events.
8	Identify events where the user chose to ignore an item.	AV-Treatment	Report AV recommended action bypass attempts.
9	Identify events of the applications that were quarantined and restored.	AV-Treatment	Detect failed quarantine-restore attempts.

Table 19 Recommended Use Cases and Correlation Rules

End-point Threat Protection / Application Control / Whitelisting solution

End-point security monitoring tools are used for prevention and detection of threats against the devices which they are running on. Though the threat visibility of the attack is limited the end-point devices communicate with its server to share information about the data. So, this makes it important to monitor end-point security server and client event data. SIEM boxes should have policies to correlate activities on end points servers and clients.

Application white listing solutions allows the execution of specific application based on defined policies related to users, groups, systems and other attributes. The trust worthiness of an application can be determined by verifying the software vendors trusted certificates or with the path value used by the applications. Legitimacy of an application can also be checked with the hash values of files affiliated with an application using common hashing protocols.

Behavior analytics also plays a considerable role in the detection of rogue applications. It is not easy to define generic use cases for this kind of event sources. The features offered by the solutions should be analyzed case by case for developing effective use cases.

Recommended Use Cases and Correlation Rules

Sl. No.	Use Case	Event Type	Correlation
1	To identify & prevent the use of unauthorized software in enterprise environment. Detect the malicious software implantation, propagation, scanning & intrusion nearly real time.	Rogue Software	Installation of unauthorized software and the use of rogue applications
2	Detect & prevent zero day attack initiation & progress in enterprise environment nearly real time.	Zero Day	Detect possible zero day attack initiation.
3	To identify the data access attempts & to prevent the data loss by strict monitoring of files, directories, USB's & other removable devices.	External devices	Detect possible data exfiltration attempts. Top and unusual Web and database application access.

Sl. No.	Use Case	Event Type	Correlation
4	Detect & prevent malicious software infection / propagation from USB's & other removable devices.	External devices	Detect unauthorized removable device in use
5	To monitor access requests to fixed-function end-point devices, such as point-of-sale (POS), medical equipment, Industrial control systems, SCADA, aeronautical system & to prevent unauthorized access attempts.	PoS	Detect unauthorized access attempts to fixed-functions in end points
6	To perform user / Administrator activity monitoring & to ensure compliance.	UAM	Detect unusual user activity

Sl. No.	Use Case	Event Type	Correlation
7	To perform malware impact assessment to aid investigation with details like time & type of attack, mode of propagation, which endpoints have been infected and which machines are engaged in suspicious activity.	Impact Assessment	Detect suspicious end point activity

Table 20 End-point threat protection / Application control / Whitelisting solution - Recommended Use Cases and Correlation Rules

Web / Application Server or Database

Enterprises use web applications for quick, user friendly and effortless access to cooperate data. Most of the time applications are installed on top of common web server solutions like IIS or Apache. These servers may be laden with vulnerabilities and should be patched and monitored to avoid security risks. Attackers use specially crafted SQL, LDAP and other commands to access web application server database content. Though secure coding practices like strict input validation, exception management, data encoding and data escaping helps to minimize the threats web application server is exposed to, it is crucial to capture and report each possible attack.

Integration of database access monitoring (DAM) application to SIEM is a prevalent best practice now. All database transactions are captured and alerts are generated for possible policy violation attempts. Sensitive data access monitoring is enabled near real time by this.

Recommended Use Cases and Correlation Rules

Sl. No.	Use Case	Event Type	Correlation
1	Monitor web server and web middleware application logs to detect ATYPICAL events.	Database Activity	Web application attacks per server and application. Web application attacks remediated. Top web application attack by type, by source, by destination. Web application attacks not remediated. Web and database platform configuration changes. Web and database platform outages due to configuration changes. Application platform resource utilization anomalies. Database application security issues / trends. Database queries, inserts or deletes that are Atypical. Excessive denied requests by web application by source/ destination. Web application errors by application type. Top Critical SQL commands by administrator. Top monitored database table attribute changes. Top and unusual Web and database application access. Top Web application administrative changes. Top or Unusual application process or resource utilization by application server. Web application outages associated with attacks or configuration changes.

Table 21 Web/Application Server or Database - Recommended Use Cases and Correlation Rules

Data Loss Prevention / File Integrity Monitor

Data exfiltration attempts can be identified and prevented with DLP solutions. Network security teams are struggling with DLP solutions integrated with SIEM, the underlying problem is "attempt to manage SIEM and DLP "separately without seeing them as products part of the "securing monitoring" process. DLP prevent end users from uploading sensitive corporate information to internet through email, cloud storage and other applications. Proper data classification is very much needed for the working of DLP. It is always a fair best practice to review the data classification and alert settings of your DLP before integrating it with your SIEM. This practice will help you to prevent problems with the false alerts generated by DLP. The combination of SIEM and DLP helps organizations in implementing effective security monitoring for compliance violation detection. It helps organizations understand and manage the data that is used, stored and transmitted. It is also useful for PCI-DSS monitoring. By integrating DLP with SIEM organizations can have security analytics in one program. It is also critical to tune your SIEM to focus on where the data is found, doing so helps the network security team responsible for managing the infrastructure protect the sensitive data at the source, in transit and at its destination. SIEM can also play a major role in alerting the DLP about new sensitive resources and the threat to organizations. Improved visibility and control is one of the immediate benefits of integrating SIEM with DLP. Regulatory compliance standards like PCI, SOX, HIPA, GLBA etc. demands confidential information and intellectual property protection and detection of such breaches.

A DLP solutions can detect different kinds of data losses like:

1) Unintentional data leakage by an internal employee.
2) Intentional data theft by an internal employee.
3) Determined data theft by skilled internal employees, external hackers and advanced persist threats or malware.

A DLP system should be capable of dealing with all the three stage of data:

1) Data in use (end points)
2) Data in motion (network)
3) Data in rest (storage)

Data stored in end points can be exfilterated via USB, email, webmail, http, instant messenger, FTP etc. The data in motion exfiltration can be through SMTP, FTP, HTTP etc. The data at rest could be accessed or owned by a wrong person or can reside at a completely wrong place. A DLP mechanism for data in use or data in motion may monitor data flows from sources like a user, an end-point, an email address or a group of them to destinations like an end-point, an email address or a group of them through channels like USB, email or network protocol.

For data exfiltration detection of data at rest a DLP solution may install a discovery agent locally. For this you may need to specify what is sensitive data and the authorized sources to handle it.

Recommended Use Cases and Correlation Rules

Sl. No.	Use Case	Event type	Correlation Rule
1	To determine where data is stored across endpoints and servers. To identify true data owners and detect unusual activities. To monitor Customer Data in transit through & off the corporate network.	Data	Detect possible data exfiltration attempt. Potential sensitive data disclosure. Violations by category

Sl. No.	Use Case	Event type	Correlation Rule
2	To monitor sensitive Intellectual Property data in transit through & off the corporate network. To monitor sensitive Corporate Data in transit through & off the corporate network.	Data	Detect Intellectual Property exfiltration attempt.
3	To monitor changes to the sensitive data in storage.	Data	Detect possible data corruption attempt.
4	Detect policy violations related to the transmission of sensitive data.	Data	Detect possible data exfiltration attempt.
5	Detect sensitive data sent over IPV6.	Data	Detect possible data exfiltration attempt.

Sl. No.	Use Case	Event type	Correlation Rule
6	Detect in-motion data leakage over the web and through email, with DLP policy rules that include content, context, and destination.	Policies	Detect possible data exfiltration attempt.
7	To analyse events related to encryption & decryption of backup tapes and other storage devices.	Confidentiality	Detect possible data confidentiality violation attempt.
8	To identify unauthorized physical or network access, malware, end-user actions that may result in data loss.	Threats	Detect possible data exfiltration attempt.

Sl. No.	Use Case	Event type	Correlation Rule
9	To analyse DLP end-point policy enforcements to prevent information leak.	Data	Detect possible data exfiltration attempt. System Access outside business hours. Top Resource access failure per user.
10	To analyse security events reported on copying of data to removable storage devices and media.	Data	Detect possible data exfiltration attempt. Top users with DLP incidents.

Table 22 Data Loss Prevention / File Integrity Monitor - Recommended Use Cases and Correlation Rules

Financial Application

Modern day SIEM solutions offer seemingly less application monitoring of financial systems. Some financial application like Cleartouch from FISERV collect customer data such as credit and debit card numbers and bank PINs. Moreover, such applications centralize the business actions and allow multiple departments access to the data. Employees who have access to this kind of data only need a fraction of it for their work functions. Knowing exactly who is doing what with this kind of data is critical for preventing security breaches.

Some of the financial service applications collect PII (Personal Identifiable Information) like social security number, mobile number etc. In order to avoid possible mishaps with such sensitive information, a company should monitor the use of it. Organizations use dedicated privilege user application monitoring solutions to monitor their internal storage activities related to financial applications. Integrating PUM (Privileged User Activity Monitoring) with SIEM helps organizations ensure the security and confidentially of customer records and offers protection against all anticipated threats to the integrity of such records and minimizes the inconvenience to the customer.

Recommended Use Cases and Correlation Rules

Sl. No.	Use Case	Event Type	Correlation Rule
1	To ensure that Secure Sockets Layer (SSL) is in use for all sensitive web application data access requests related to procurement, purchasing, making payment, Customer Orders, Order fulfilment and receiving payment from Customers.	Confidentiality	Detect sensitive data transfer over unsecure communication channel.
2	To ensure that all the common end-point protection tools are there in place & is in a properly protected state.	Controls	Detect current end point security posture.

Sl. No.	Use Case	Event Type	Correlation Rule
3	To ensure that operating attack surface on all clients and servers accessing critical financial systems are reduced.	Attack	Detect intrusion attempts on financial applications.
4	To analyse the databases monitoring events and auditing software events reported by financial & accounting applications.	Monitoring	Detect unusual application access attempts. Administrative access to Critical system outside normal business hours.
5	To analyse user logon/logoff reports (log-in/log-out monitoring) of financial and accounting applications.	User	Detect unusual application access attempts.

Sl. No.	Use Case	Event Type	Correlation Rule
6	To analyse the Log-on Failure Reports of financial & accounting applications.	User Access	Detect unusual application access attempts.
7	To analyse the Audit Logs Access events to financial & accounting applications.	User Access	Detect unusual application access attempts
8	Identify when an object like File, Directory, etc. related to financial & accounting applications is accessed, the type of access (RO/RW) and whether or not access was successful/failed, and who performed the action.	User Access	Detect unusual application access attempts

Sl. No.	Use Case	Event Type	Correlation Rule
9	Analyse local system processes such as system start up and shutdown and changes to the system time or audit log.	System	Detect unusual application access attempts.
10	Analyse event logs for changes in the security configuration settings such as adding or removing a global or local group, adding or removing members from a global or local group, etc.	System	Detect unusual application access attempts.
11	To analyse the status of internal controls in place for accessing financial & accounting applications.	Controls	Detect unusual application access attempts. Unusual access using service account credentials.

Table 23 Financial Application

Host Based Firewall

Host based firewall are designed for protection against security threats originating from LAN environments and can help mitigate the risks of an end-point host. Host based firewall are also known as personal firewalls. The host based firewalls are software modules installed on each individual end-point systems. Most of the personal firewalls offer protection beyond capabilities of a network firewall. It protects end points system from Trojans, spywares and other malicious software. it is typically useful for roaming end users who cannot always be connected to the internet through a hardware firewall. Most of the modern-day operating system comes with integrated personal firewall. However, we cannot expect rich features of a commercial personal firewall from this. Personal firewalls are not a replacement for antivirus solutions. Zone Alarm, Tiny personal firewall, KERIO etc. are examples of commonly used personal firewall solutions.

A well configured personal firewall provides effective protection against different kinds of attacks. Continuously monitoring the personal firewall logs with security monitoring solutions like SIEM is a good idea to detect potential compromises in end-point machines. The internal firewall rules configured in personal firewalls acts as a simple access control list with logging capability. Port scanning activities and malicious software implementation can be identified near real time with the integration of personal firewall with SIEM.

Event Categories

1) Antivirus – Most of the Host based firewalls has AV capabilities.
2) IDS/IPS – Host based Firewalls use IDS/ IPS engines for deep inspection.
3) Phishing - Protects the end users from going to phishing websites.
4) Intrusion - Protects end systems from targeted attacks.
5) Data - Monitors data in transit & prevents the malicious data transfer.

Recommended Use Cases and Correlation Rules

Sl. No.	Use Cases	Event Type	Correlation Rule
1	All Antivirus Use Cases.	AV	All AV correlation rules.
2	All Intrusion Detection/Prevention System Use Cases.	IDS/ IPS	All IDS/IPS correlation rules.

Sl. No.	Use Cases	Event Type	Correlation Rule
3	Identify the phishing sites accessed by the end user.	Phishing	Suspicious web communication, possible PHISHING attempt.
4	Detect targeted attacks from local networks & internet.	Intrusion	Targeted attack detected.
5	To monitor the system for real-time program activity and connection status.	System	Top System connections.
6	To identify "calling home" attempts by malware for transmitting sensitive data to hackers.	Data	Top source and destinations of malicious connections. Detect C & C communication in progress.
7	To identify attempts to modify critical system & application files.	Data	Critical file access, possible data corruption or exfiltration attempt.

Sl. No.	Use Cases	Event Type	Correlation Rule
8	To identify the user attempts for privilege escalation.	System	Detect Privilege escalation attempts possible system intrusion. Authentication failures by privileged user
9	To identify the attempts for service status modification by processes/users.	System	Service modification request, possible Rootkit implantation
10	Identify the request by application for attributes associated with the processing environment.	System	Reconnaissance or possible information gathering attempt

Table 24 Host Based Firewall - Recommended Use Cases and Correlation Rules

Single Sign-On Solution

Single Sign On (SSO) permits a user to access all the computer resources where he has access permission through a single process of authentication. SSO reduces the human error and inconvenience issues caused by typing in the user credential multiple times. SSO is a difficult to implement technology. Novell's SSO solution works slight different than other SSO solutions. They store the separate user names and passwords of different applications in a common store called SecretStore. Solutions like Open-AM SSO uses HTTP cookies to track user actions. Single Sign On permits to terminate user access to multiple software application with a single action of sign-out.

Benefits of SSO

1) Reduced errors and operating failures.
2) Improved security with a single user authentication.
3) Reduced administrative efforts in managing user accounts.
4) Consistent and reliable performance.

Though there are multiple benefits with single sign on it is important to note down that an SSO solution is a very attractive target for a hacker to perform denial of service attacks. SSO is an expensive retrofit solution to an existing application. The single point of failure nature and the risk associated with unattended end user system that uses SSO should also be considered while designing the integrated monitoring solution with SSO.

Recommended Use Cases and Correlation Rules

Sl. No.	Use Case	Event Type	Correlation Rule
1	To identify & analyse the Auto-provisioning of user accounts by IM solution & to verify the privilege level assigned to each.	Auto-provisioning	Suspicious user account provisioning or modifications.
2	To identify & analyse the Auto-de-activation of user accounts by IM solution.	Auto-de-activation	Suspicious user account deactivations or modifications.
3	To analyse the Identity-synchronization events reported by IM solution.	Identity-synchronization	Suspicious user account attribute changes
4	To verify & analyse the self-service requests events reported by IM solution.	self-service requests	Suspicious user account service requests.

Sl. No.	Use Case	Event Type	Correlation Rule
5	To verify analyse the modification of users & entitlements reported by IM solution.	Delegated- administration	Suspicious user account modifications.
6	To analyse propagation of changes from one system to other.	propagation of changes	Track propagation of user account changes.
7	To analyse user requests for change of their own or others' profiles and requests for additional access rights.	Profiles	Suspicious User Profile modifications.
8	To analyse automatic discovery and classification of systems and accounts by IM solution.	Discovery	Detect rogue system & user accounts
9	To verify the orphaned accounts.	Orphan	Report unused or Orphaned accounts

Sl. No.	Use Case	Event Type	Correlation Rule
10	To verify the privileges assigned to each user by IM solution.	inappropriate privileges	Track inappropriate privileges assignments.
11	To verify the multiple privileges assigned to user accounts by IM solution.	Privilege	Violation of separation of duties.
12	To analyse the Duplication of information Identity information stored in IM solutions.	Duplication	Identity data duplication.
13	To verify & analyse the single sign-on events reported by IM solution.	SSO	ATYPICAL SSO incidents.

Table 25 Single Sign-On Solution - Recommended Use Cases and Correlation Rules

Intrusion Detection/Prevention System

The basic difference between IDS and IPS is the fact

that IDS focuses only on detection and IPS can take actions along with the detection. IDS can passively monitor more than one segment and can monitor traffic that an IPS would never see. IPS actions include drop, reset, shun or custom actions, and it is placed in line with the traffic for taking this action. The "fail open" feature of IPS allows traffic to pass through in case of IPS engine or scan failure. Modern day firewalls come with software modules or hardware daughter cards for IPS/IDS feature. UTM boxes will also have IPS/IDS features in built. For effective security monitoring of firewall events the below set of use cases are recommended.

Recommended Use Cases and Correlation Rules

Sl. No.	Use Case	Event Type	Correlation Rule
1	To identify attacks targeting vulnerabilities in operating systems and applications.	Vulnerabilities	Known vulnerability exploitation attempt

Sl. No.	Use Case	Event Type	Correlation Rule
2	Detect botnet events used to perform targeted Denial of Service (DoS) attacks or steal personally identifiable information (PII)	DOS/ PII	PII data ex-filtration
3	Detect both known and unknown threats by comparing the behaviour with the predefined rule set. Detect incidents by comparing traffic patterns that the IPS considers "normal" with new traffic patterns, and deciding whether new traffic patterns fall within acceptable patterns or not.	Rules	Suspicious or unusual incidents

Sl. No.	Use Case	Event Type	Correlation Rule
4	To identify ineffective IPS rule or signature that results in False Positive alarms/actions. To identify ineffective IPS rule or signature that results in False Negative alarms/actions.		Top False Alarms
5	To identify worms that exploit a vulnerability to install itself, scans the network for additional potential victims and self-propagate from one computer to the next.		Worm Outbreaks
6	To identify Trojan's that propagate itself from system to system with human intervention.	Trojans	Trojan propagation
7	To identify buffer overflow attacks against applications & systems.	DOS	Dos or Buffer overflows

Sl. No.	Use Case	Event Type	Correlation Rule
8	To identify scanning , fingerprinting & enumeration attempts against the corporate network or resources by attackers.	Scan	Unusual scanner / probe activities
9	To identify spywares that tracks sites visited with a browser, records keystrokes and mouse clicks & change browser settings to obtain information from computers.	Spyware	User activity monitoring & data capturing by spyware
10	Detect phishing attempts where scammer sends large quantities of genuine-looking e-mail messages to intended victims in an effort to entice them to open an attachment or click a URL.	Phishing	Email Spear Phishing attempts

Sl. No.	Use Case	Event Type	Correlation Rule
11	Detect SYN Floods and Denial of Service (DoS) Attacks against corporate resources.	DOS	DoS Attacks
12	To identify the obfuscation attempts by attacker.	EVA-SION	Obfuscation/Evasion attempt
13	To identify the tunnelled & encrypted malicious data transfer.	EVA-SION	Data exfiltration over secure channels
14	To identify the attackers attempt to send malicious network packets in smaller fragments.	EVA-SION	Fragmented data Exfiltration attempt
15	To identify the attackers attempt to send malicious network packets as protocol specific data.	EVA-SION	Suspicious protocol traffic

Table 26 Intrusion Detection/Prevention System - Recommended Use Cases and Correlation Rules

Network Based Firewall

Firewall is an access control device which decides which traffic to forward and which traffic not to forward, based on the pre-defined rules. Firewalls screen both inbound and outbound network traffic.

The major features of an enterprise grade network firewall include:

1) Blocking the incoming traffic based on source or destination IP or port.
2) Blocking the outgoing traffic based on source or destination IP or port.
3) Screen network traffic for unacceptable and inappropriate content.
4) Enable remote access of resources.
5) Allow connection to internal network.
6) Generates alerts on network activities.

Firewall Technologies
Packet Filtering

Packet filtering works at the network layer of OSI model. The filtering is based on service type, port number, interface number, source /destination address etc.

Network Address Translation (NAT)

Network address translation (NAT) enables mapping of internal private IP address to external public IP addresses. A firewall can perform one to one or many to one static or dynamic mapping.

Circuit Level Gateways

These are firewall which works under session layer of OSI model. Multiple parameters like address, DNS name, Directory name etc. are used for allowing or denying network access.

Application Proxies

It works as a proxy server that intercepts information passing through the gateway and thus does not allow direct communication. Application proxies will allow a limited number of applications like FTP, SMTP etc.

Virtual Private Network

Most of the modern-day network firewalls act as VPN termination points. This kind of firewall support both site to site and remote access virtual private network connection.

FW Logs - Common Categories

1. Firewall change management Logs
2. Firewall bandwidth monitoring alerts

3. Firewall Internet / Intranet Usage alerts (Permitted and Blocked)
4. Firewall IPSEC/SSL/Tunnel/Point to Point

Recommended Use Cases and Correlation Rules

Sl. No.	Use Cases	Event Type	Correlation Rules
1	Get a complete trail of all the changes done to firewall configuration. Identify 'who' made 'what' changes, 'when' and 'why' to firewall configuration. Identify attempts to start or stop auditing service of the Firewall. Identify attempts to clear trace contents from audit log container.	Firewall change management Logs Modification of FW audit logging service. Enable FW audit logging service Disable FW audit logging service Delete audit records in FW	Changes to active and standby Firewall configuration Detect Configuration change related to firewall policies and VPN Detect Audit Log removal attempts

Sl. No.	Use Cases	Event Type	Correlation Rules
2	Monitor network traffic and generate alert notifications upon sudden spikes in bandwidth. Analyse which user, protocol group or network activity is consuming more bandwidth. Analyse the firewall logs to identify the users violating the corporate internet download/usage policy. Monitoring internet usage (overuse or misuse) by employees. Identify the protocol wise internet usage by the users. Identify the user attempts to access restricted sites. Analyse the firewall logs to identify that which VOIP phones are trying to connect to the VoIP server using TFTP to get the configurations. Detect DoS attack against the application servers by analysing the no of inbound connections to the server farm through firewall. Analyse incoming and outgoing traffic/bandwidth patterns in enterprise network. Identify top Web users, and top websites accessed	FW - Traffic and Bandwidth monitoring events

FW - Internet / Intranet Usage alerts. | Top unusual peak bandwidth utilization sources and destinations Top bandwidth by protocol, by connection, by source and by destination Top blocked internal sources by port, by destinations Top perimeter attacks by category Top dropped traffic from DMZ, FW Top blocked outbound connections by port, by destination Unusual DNS access and requests Changes to active and standby configurations by perimeter device class

Daily or weekly alerts on top 10 connections from sites of concerns |

Sl. No.	Use Cases	Event Type	Correlation Rules
4	Identify the VPN tunnel creation by the FW / VPN gateway Identify the VPN tunnel termination by the FW / VPN gateway or user. Generate alerts for file download over VPN session. Generate alerts for object/resource access over VPN session. Identify the bytes of data transferred over VPN session.	IPSEC/SSL VPN or TUNNEL initiation. IPSEC/SSL VPN or TUNNEL termination. IPSEC/SSL VPN or TUNNEL termination due to policy violation , compliance or communication issues Data transfer over IPSEC/SSL VPN or TUNNEL sessions Object/resource binding by any of the participating peer with the other over IPSEC/SSL VPN or TUNNEL sessions Release of the Object/resource binded by any of the participating peer with the other over IPSEC/SSL VPN or TUNNEL sessions Queries regarding the objects / resource access over VPN session.	

Table 27 Network Based Firewall - Recommended Use Cases
and Correlation Rules

Network User Behavior Analysis (NUBA)

NUBA offers passive monitoring of user behavior without major network reconfiguration. Continuous real time view of user activities across enterprise network is captured and monitored by the solution. The user role information in your existing directories will be used as the reference for the analysis. Some of these solutions are capable of even controlling user access based on the findings. A centralized active login data base needs to be accessible by NUBA for analysis. If needed LDAP queries will be used for verifying user or group mission. Port mirroring or passive network taps are used by the network user behavior analysis tools for deep packet inspection. Flow data like Cisco netflow, Juniper jflow etc. are used for analyzing changes made by the end users. Event data generated by network user behavior analysis tools are exported to security information event manager (SIEM) either by using SNMP, SMTP or any other protocols. Some of the NUBA tools support importing of vulnerability assessment data for relevancy check of the findings.

Popular Threat Detection Methodologies used by NUBA

Payload Anomaly Detection
Protocol Anomaly: MAC Spoofing

Protocol Anomaly: IP Spoofing
Protocol Anomaly: TCP/UDP Fanout
Protocol Anomaly: IP Fanout
Protocol Anomaly: Duplicate IP
Protocol Anomaly: Duplicate MAC
Virus Detection
Bandwidth Anomaly Detection
Connection Rate Detection

Recommended Use Cases and Correlation Rules

Sl. No.	Use Case	Event Type	Correlation Rule
1	To analyse business user behaviour and activity across the network environment.	UBA	Suspicious behaviour by source, by destination, by type
2	To analyse the environment for network usage, critical assets & to identify malfunctioning devices and detect trends	Statistics	Suspicious communication by source, by destination, by type

Sl. No.	Use Case	Event Type	Correlation Rule
3	To analyse application usage statistics, host-level audit trails or network activity, spam detection and application failure notifications.	Statistics	
4	To compare the internal behavioural analysis data with the one from perimeter devices.		
5	Detect & analyse network and security issues of specific users.	UBA	
6	To perform trend analysis of user activity with the historical behavioural data collected.	UBA	

Sl. No.	Use Case	Event Type	Correlation Rule
7	To detect and analyse Network scans, Service probes, Protocol anomalies, Network behaviour anomalies, Application behaviour anomalies, Unauthorized services detected, Unauthorized communication channels detected, Custom signature deployments & Regular and on-demand signature updates.	UBA	
8	Detect evasive threats with deep packet inspection of protocols like DHCP, AIM, DNS, FTP, HTTP, IRC, Kerberos, POP, SIP, SMTP, SSL, TLS etc.	DPI	Suspicious communications by Protocol

Sl. No.	Use Case	Event Type	Correlation Rule
9	Detect different kinds of unknown and highly customized attacks like - Zero-Day attacks – detection of zero-day attack symptoms Data leakage– misused HTTP(S), FTP, SMB Tunnelled traffic– ICMP, DNS, SSH. Protocol anomalies– detecting changes of use of common protocols and their characteristics. Mascaraed brute-force attack (dictionary, brute-force) Breach of internal security rules by employees.	Threats	Suspicious communications by Protocol

Table 28 Network User Behavior Analysis (NUBA) - Recommended Use Cases and Correlation Rules

Operating System

Almost all the SIEM solutions can receive log data directly from windows, Linux, UNIX, OSX and other operating systems. Dedicated agents like SNARE, Adaptive Log Exporter, Sentinel UNIX agent etc. are also used for exporting logs.

Modern day windows operating system offers centralized windows event log collection. This innovative server subscriber model reduces the complexity of integrating all event sources separately to SIM or SIEM. SIEM providers may offer agents or add-ons for exporting archived windows event logs. Microsoft windows management instrumentation (WMI) API can be used for remote agent less windows event log collection from windows server version 2003, 2008, Windows XP, Windows Vista and Windows 7. Windows event log protocol needs proper configuration of server DCOM settings.

Recommended Use Cases and Correlation Rules

Sl. No.	Use Cases	Event Type	Cor-relation Rule
Linux/Unix Common OS Logs			
1	To analyse general message and system related events which needs attention.	System	Detect un-usual OS incidents
	To analyze OS authenti-cation logs (Successful & Failed).	Auth	
	To analyze kernel level logs for system Panic / failure conditions.	Kernel	
	To analyze scheduled, run-ning & cancelled cron jobs.	CRON	
	To analyse system mail server logs.	MAIL	
	To analyse Apche access and error logs.	HTTPD	
	To analyse OS boot log.	BOOT	
	To analyse Lighttpd access and error logs.	Lighttpd	
	To analyse MySQL data-base server log file	Mysqld	
	To analyse login records file.	utmp/wtmp	
	To analyse yum command usage.	Yum	
	To analyse kernel ring buf-fer information.	Dmesg	

Sl. No.	Use Cases	Event Type	Correlation Rule
Linux/Unix Common OS Logs			
Windows System Events			
2	Detect & analyse the failed access requests by users & applications.	Failure Audit	Detect unusual OS incidents
	Detect &analyse the successful access requests by users & applications.	Success Audit	
	Detect &analyse warning messages by the Operating System.	Warning.	
	Detect & analyse the information logs by Operating System.	Information.	
	Detect & analyse critical OS issues.	Error	

Table 29 Operating System - Recommended Use Cases and Correlation Rules

Proxy

Proxy servers intercept the connection from endpoints to the target destination and thus limit direct connection between them. The proxies can be configured as content filtering solutions. Typically, forward proxy servers are configured as content filtering solutions. Reverse proxy servers can act as server load balancing gateways distributing the connection requests to various servers inside the server farm. Sticky connections can be configured for persistent traffic flow to specific servers inside the server farm. The logs generated by both content filtering and reverse proxy servers are relevant from security perspective. So, it is highly important to ensure the smooth integration of proxy servers with SIEM.

Types of Proxy

Gateway: A proxy server that passes requests and responses unmodified.

Forward Proxy: An Internet facing proxy used to forward requests from a wide range of sources.

Reverse Proxy: Internet-facing proxy used as a front-end to control and protect access to a server on a private network.

Event Categories

- Θ   Malware / HTTP content inspection
- Θ   Web Caching
- Θ   Forward & Reverse Proxy Content

Recommended Use Cases and Correlation Rules

Sl. No.	Use Case	Event Type	Correlation Rule
1	To analyse the Infected, Suspicious and Encrypted Files reported by malware inspection.	Malware	
	To analyze the Maximum Archive Nesting Exceeded, Maximum Size Exceeded, Maximum Unpacked File Size Exceeded events reported by the Malware Inspection Engine.	Malware/ Size Exceeded	HTTP response blocked
	To analyze the Unknown Encoding, Corrupted File & Time Out events reported by the Malware Inspection Engine.	Malware/ File	HTTP response blocked
	To analyse Malware Inspection Disabled, Malware Inspection Disabled for the Matching Policy Rule, Malware Inspection Disabled for the Matching Web Chaining Rule, Destination Included in Malware Inspection Exceptions List, Response Originated from Proxy Server, Request denied by Malware Inspection Web Filter, Request/Response pair Identified as Exempted Protocol Message & Response Identified as a 200 Response to a CONNECT Request events reported by the Malware Inspection Engine.	Malware/Inspection Status	Malware inspection bypass
2	Identify the frequently accessed web pages by analysing the Proxy Cache Logs.	Cache	Top web pages served

Sl. No.	Use Case	Event Type	Correlation Rule
3	Forward & Reverse Proxy Content Filtering. • Analyse the Proxy logs to identify the users violating the corporate internet download/usage policies. • Monitoring internet usage (overuse or misuse) of employees. • Identify the protocol wise internet usage by the users. • Identify the user attempts to access restricted & malicious websites • Detect DoS attack against the application servers by analysing the no of inbound connections to the server farm through reverse proxy server. •Analyse incoming and outgoing traffic/bandwidth patterns in enterprise network. • Identify top web users, and top websites accessed. • Identify the user attempts to access adult websites. • To analyse the cached objected served by the Proxy server. • Information about requests and responses provided by the Internet web servers • To identify the category wise internet usage. • To analyse access times for various categories of requests. • To identify the policy rules that either allowed or denied access to the request.	PROXY -Content Filtering alerts	Internet usage policy violations Top inbound connections to internal sources by system, user, bandwidth and time. Top outbound connections to external sources by system, user, bandwidth and time. Top outbound DMZ connections to external sources by system, user, bandwidth and time. Bandwidth over consumption. Blocked website access requests

Table 30 Proxy - Recommended Use Cases and Correlation Rules

Storage

All authorized and unauthorized access requests to storage solutions should be monitored by integrating it with a SIEM solution. Below list does not address all the relevant storage use cases a security analyst should develop, however at least this much of uses cases should be there in the SIEM for proper security monitoring.

Recommended Use Cases and Correlation Rules

Sl. No.	Use Case	Event Type	Correlation Rules
1	Detect Zone hopping attacks that targets FC switch weaknesses.	Attack	Fiber Channel Targeted Attacks
2	LUN masking attacks/ WWN spoofing that targets HBA weaknesses.	Attack	LUN targeted Attacks
3	Detect SAN Name server pollution attacks targets FLOGI/PLOGI weaknesses.	Attack	LUN targeted Attacks
4	Detect SAN Man-in-the-Middle attacks that targets Fabric address weaknesses.	Attack	SAN MiTM Attacks

Sl. No.	Use Case	Event Type	Correlation Rules
5	Detect SAN Session hijacking attacks that targets Fibre Channel frame weaknesses.	Attack	SAN session hijacking
6	To analyses the reallocation scans performed recently.	Operation	Suspicious reallocation scans
7	To analyse the storage systems audit logs for Start & Stop of Audit service & attempt for deletion & modification of audit entries. What configuration files were accessed? When the configuration files were accessed? What has been changed in the configuration files? What commands were executed? Who executed the commands? & When the commands were executed?		Storage audit trail corruption

Sl. No.	Use Case	Event Type	Correlation Rules
8	Detect & analyse "forged ICMP redirect" attacks against the storage.	Attack	Storage - "forged ICMP redirect" attacks
9	To analyse the "ping throttling threshold" events reported by the storage solution.	Attack	Storage - "ping throttling threshold"
10	To analyse "Excessive un-supported protocol packets" are being sent to storage system.	Attack	Excessive unsup-ported protocol packets
11	To analyse the "excessive embryonic TCP connection drops" reported by storage system.	Attack	Excessive embryonic TCP connection drops
12	To identify whether there is any cardholder data or PII stored. To identify whether there is any sensitive authentica-tion data contained in the payment card's storage chip or full magnetic stripe. To identify whether there is any payment card data in payment card terminals or other unprotected endpoint devices, such as PCs, laptops or smart phones.	Data Storage	PCI DSS data stor-age violation
13	Detect protocol wise access details of the data in storage.	Access	Protocol wise data access

Table 31 Storage - Recommended Use Cases and Correlation Rules

Virtual Private Network

Virtual Private Network gateways provide secure end to end connections between end points. They act as a termination point of secure connection from both static and dynamic end points. Site to Site (S2S) or LAN to LAN VPN connections are always up secure tunnels between gateways. Most of the modern-day firewalls will have VPN capabilities. SSL/TLS, IPSEC etc. are commonly used protocols for VPN. Out of this SSL or TLS based VPN is used for secure dynamic connections from roaming endpoints. IPSEC is a suite of protocols that offers confidentiality and integrity for secure VPN connection. ISAKMP, ESP, AH etc. are the commonly used protocols for IPSEC.ISAKMP is responsible for maintenance and termination of a secure channel over unsecure medium. Data is sent over the secure channel built by ISAKMP with additional protection of ESP or AH.ESP offers both confidentially and integrity services. You may setup VPN with ESP alone or by using a combination of ESP and AH for data protection. To have better visibility of VPN activities you need to integrate VPN gateways with SIEM.SSL multiplexers either integrated within firewall or running in separate gateways split the SSL or HTTPS connection packet inspection. You may integrate SSL multiplexers with your security analytics solutions for improved visibility of events related to data sent over secure SSL/HTTPS channel.

Recommended Use Cases and Correlation Rules

Sl. No.	Use Case	Event Type	Correlation Rules
1	Identify & Analyse the frequent IKE negotiation failures on the Remote access VPN GW. Identify & Analyse the authentication failures on the Remote access VPN GW. Identify & Analyse multiple denials and successful logins on remote access VPN GW. Identify & Analyse targeted SSL vulnerability attacks on VPN GW's. Identify attacks on IPSEC VPN Gateways configured with aggressive mode. Alert when a virus, spyware or other malware is detected by end-point assessment module of VPN Gateway on a host. Alert when end-point assessment module of VPN Gateway successfully removes a piece of malware on an end host.	VPN reconnaissance /Attack	Targeted SSL vulnerability attacks on VPN GW's Top successful logins to VPN GW Top failed logins to VPN GW IKE Negotiation failures

Sl. No.	Use Case	Event Type	Correlation Rules
2	Alert when a virus, spyware or other malware is detected by end-point assessment module of VPN Gateway on a host. Alert when end-point assessment module of VPN Gateway successfully removes a piece of malware on an end host. Alert when end-point assessment module of VPN Gateway successfully removes a piece of malware on an end host.	Endpoint AV SCAN	Failed endpoint assessments by VPN GW
3	Identify the VPN tunnel creation by the FW / VPN gateway. Identify the VPN tunnel termination by the FW / VPN gateway or user. Generate alerts for file download over VPN session. Generate alerts for object/resource access over VPN session. Identify the bytes of data transferred over VPN session.	Data transfer	Suspicious data transfer over VPN session

Table 32 Virtual Private Network - Recommended Use Cases and Correlation Rules

Vulnerability Scanner

Timely detection of threats by an SIEM can be enhanced with its integration with vulnerability manager. Relevancy of an identified threat can be verified with the vulnerability data. The overall accuracy of threat detection is thus improved with this integration. Vulnerability management solutions or scanners are added as event sources in SIEM, in addition to the relevancy checking the below set of use cases will help the security analyst in real time threat detection when the vulnerability scanning happens.

Recommended Use Cases and Correlation Rules

Sl. No.	Use Cases	Event Type	Correlation Rules
1	To analyse the asset enumeration status provided by the VA tool.	Enumeration and Fingerprinting	NA
2	To analyse the profiling data of network assets by VA tool. Offline configuration auditing of network devices.	Profiling	NA

Sl. No.	Use Cases	Event Type	Correlation Rules
3	To identify the patch auditing status of the enterprise network	Patch Status	Systems without approved patches
4	To analyses Control Systems Auditing data.	Audit Status	
5	To analyse the PII (personally identifiable information) data stored in enterprise networks.	PII	PII (Personal Identity Information) data storage violations
6	To identify threats like Botnet/Malicious Process, Virus, Worm, Trojan and to analyse the vulnerabilities exist in Web Applications.	Threats	Vulnerability to incident ratio and vulnerability trends. Attacks against vulnerable systems classified by criticality.

Sl. No.	Use Cases	Event Type	Correlation Rules
7	To check the compliance status of the environment.	Compliance	Compliance violations.
8	To check the configuration auditing status of the environment.	Configuration	Configuration Audit Report.

Table 33 Vulnerability Scanner - Recommended Use Cases and Correlation Rules

Module 6
Cyber Threat
Intelligence Basics

What is Cyber Threat Intelligence?

Today's cyber attackers are more erudite than ever. To predict and respond to their attacks, you need to understand their impetuses, intents, characteristics, and methods. Legacy, signature-based threat data feeds, can't deliver those insights. But, Cyber Threat Intelligence can.

In every major data breach that has been recorded, the victimized organizations had lots of security tools and staff. Yet they were hit hard - losing billions of customers' personal data in the process. Thus, it's clear that you cannot rely on the traditional cyber-security approach to assure your data is protected. In fact, nearly 75% of cyber attacks occur undetected. And once they are detected, it's always too late! Rather than waiting until you know you've been breached, get proactive with Cyber Threat Intelligence.

Cyber Threat Intelligence is evidence-based refined information that detects looming threats to your organization and helps alleviate your exposures to them. An effectual Cyber Threat Intelligence security team scrutinizes and prioritizes targeted and global threats, so that your organization can proactively thwart security attacks. To sum up, Cyber Threat Intelligence (CTI), also known as Threat Intelligence, is knowledge that helps you identify security threats and make informed decisions in advance.

Generally, CTI is based on the collection of intelligence using social media intelligence (SOCMINT), human Intelligence (HUMINT), open source intelligence (OSINT) or intelligence from the deep and dark network. CTI's key mission is to investigate and analyze trends and technical progresses in three areas including: Cybercrime, Cyber activism, and Cyber espionage.

Considering the stern impacts of cyber threats, CTI has emerged as an effective solution to maintain international security. The primary purpose of CTI is to help organizations understand the risks of the most common and severe external threats, such as advanced persistent threats (APTs), zero-day threats and exploits.

Types of Cyber Threat Intelligence

CTI is commonly deployed across three levels in an organisation - Tactical, Operational and Strategic levels. Let's have a look at these levels in detail.

Tactical Intelligence

Tactical Cyber Threat Intelligence is predominantly focused around a quick and immediate response. Up-to-date information and sufficient resources from operations are essential for this area of intelligence to be successful. Tactical intelligence provides support for day-to-day events and operations such as the development of signatures and indicators of compromise (IOC). Firewalls, protection systems along with anti-virus and prevention systems are all vital technologies within this layer of intelligence.

Operational Intelligence

Operational Cyber Threat Intelligence provides technically-focused, highly specialized intelligence to guide and support the response to specific incidents. The contextual level within this form of intelligence focuses profoundly on providing information about the attacker; normally identifying who, when, why and how. Other aspects such as how the attack would impact an organization strategically are also inspected. Such intelligence is most frequently used by an organization to decide its precedence, as well as form context and provide the resources for an appropriate response.

Strategic Intelligence

This layer of intelligence typically states the predominant goals that an organisation wishes to accomplish. Strategic Cyber Threat Intelligence forms an overall picture of the capabilities and the intent of pernicious cyber threats, through the identification of patterns, trends and emerging risks, in order to inform policy and decision makers or to provide timely warnings. Also, Strategic Intelligence is most appropriately used to detect potential new threats that are emerging as well as identify new technologies and how they can be used to benefit the organisation.

Key Features of Threat Intelligence Services

Data Feeds

Several types of data feeds are available through Cyber Threat Intelligence services. Examples include malicious domains/URLs, phishing URLs, IP addresses, malware hashes and many more. A vendor's Threat Intelligence feeds should draw data from its own global database, open source data as well as from industry groups, to produce a pool of data that is both deep and broad.

Alerts and Reports

Some Threat Intelligence services provide actual time alerts along with daily, weekly, monthly and quarterly threat reports. Intelligence may comprise information about emerging threats, specific types of malware and threat actors and their motives.

Benefits of Cyber Threat Intelligence

With every successful cyber-attack, the significance of real-time Cyber Threat Intelligence becomes more evident. Through Threat Intelligence, organizations can expand their visibility and insight into active and potential threats. However, there are several potential benefits of Threat Intelligence and these include:

Rich Threat Context for Faster Prioritization and Quick Response

There are multiple alerts from sources such as firewall, SIEM and other tools, Security Ops and Incident Response teams will quickly understand the seriousness of threats and try to tackle it first. Cyber Threat Intelligence provides the teams with the necessary context demonstrating what the threat is/or which category it belongs to, when was it first discovered, severity level, etc.

Leverage Network Intelligence to Identify Infected Devices

DHCP (Dynamic Host Configuration Protocol), DNS (Domain Name System) and IP Address Management services provide critical, actionable network intelligence services such as the devices used, IP addresses allocated to, and websites visited by users etc. By combining user and network context with Threat Intelligence, organizations can quickly identify infected devices and the users being targeted.

Streamline Security Operations Resources

With the shortage of cyber security professionals and the emerging threat of data breach, organizations cannot depend on scarce security resources to deflect threats. By deploying Cyber Threat Intelligence on various security systems and network control points, which is both reliable and automatically refreshed by the Threat Intelligence provider itself, organizations are free from the issue of scarce security resources.

Despite the potential benefits of Cyber Threat

Intelligence, organizations also face some key challenges, including:

- Lack of sufficient threat context
- Triaging false positive threat indicators.
- Not being able to share information internally in organized manner.
- Overcoming gaps in Threat Intelligence data.
- Complications in deploying and handling Threat Intelligence data.

Cyber Threat Intelligence Cycle

For creating a better Cyber Threat Intelligence, the security team should examine existing and predicted security threats, identify malware, exploits, threat actors, vulnerabilities and other compromise indicators in an organizational landscape. Each area of Threat Intelligence has a diverse scope of mission, which by default would require a different set of tools. Based on the area of focus, the team should execute the following cycle of operations:

- Requirements gathering
- Data Collection
- Data Processing
- Analysis and deriving intelligence
- Distribution
- Action plan and execution

To defend against today's sophisticated attackers, enterprise data security programs need to be flexible enough to include new that improve decision making. Adding Threat Intelligence to an information security program, whether through an internal capability or from a service provider, helps organizations triage security activities and focus on the areas that are most likely to stop attackers.

Advantages of CTI

Cyber Threat Intelligence (CTI) is becoming a vital component in an organization's overall risk mitigation strategy. Threat Intelligence includes indicators of compromise, tactics, procedures and techniques used by threat actors to detect and prevent emerging or existing attacks. Currently, Threat Intelligence is increasingly used by organizations tactically and operationally in response to a range of threats. However, below are the benefits of Cyber Threat Intelligence at various levels – Tactical, Operational and Strategic level.

Benefits of Tactical Threat Intelligence

- Empowers enterprises to develop a proactive cyber security posture and enhances their overall risk management policies.

- Enhances threat detection and prioritizes indicators so that analysts can rapidly identify potential events.

- Provides context to a tremendous amount of data and removes invalid indicators in order to lessen false positives.

- Provides an intelligence-led approach to your cyber security operations more quickly and accurately.

Benefits of Operational Threat Intelligence

- Provides situational awareness and context that helps Incident responders to find out attackers' intentions, targets and methods.

- Reduces incident response times through contextualization of incidents with Threat Intelligence.

- Allows Incident Responders and forensics teams to quickly mitigate damage caused by breaches and proactively protect the business from advanced threats.

Benefits of Strategic Threat Intelligence

- Efficaciously assesses, explains, and quantifies risk to senior managers and other key stakeholders to drive strategic decision making.

- Describes general attacker trends, long-term

plans and strategies including their tactics, techniques, procedures, tools preferred, and industries targeted.

- Reduces the exposure of the business to regulatory or legal sanctions.

- Demonstrates an appropriate standard of diligence to regulators, auditors and stakeholders.

While organizations face threats that are increasingly effective and complex, the time frames in which threat analysis, detection and mitigation are played out are increasingly trampled. To that end, Threat Intelligence continues to play a pivotal role in today's security efforts. All three levels of Cyber Threat Intelligence help drive decisions and ultimate results, at different levels within the business.

Module 7
Indicators of Compromise

Indicators of Compromise

For the past few years, the security industry has become more reliant on Indicators of Compromise (IOCs), since thye act as a mode to deduct targeted intrusions and adversaries. Indicators of compromise are an artifact observed in an operating system or on a network that are likely to indicate a computer intrusion. IOCs may be composed of some combination of filenames, IP addresses, hostnames, processes, services, Windows registry entries, hashes, and a host of other similar information.

In pursuit of more rapid detection of data breaches, indicators of compromise act as important breadcrumbs for security professionals inspecting their IT environments. By monitoring for indicators of compromise, organizations can detect malware attacks and act quickly so as to prevent eventual breaches from occurring or atleast stop them in their earliest stages. However, indicators of compromise are not always easy to detect; they can be as simple as metadata elements or incredibly difficult as malicious code and content samples. Analysts often identify numerous IOCs to look for correlation and piece them together to scrutinize a potential threat or incident. IOCs contain threat information that are constantly being updated and cover many domains such as:

- Threat assessment and characterization
- Malware characterization

- Cyber situational awareness
- Operational event management Logging
- Incident response
- Forensics and much more.

Why are Indicators of Compromise Important?

IOCs are significant for two main reasons. Firstly, they allow a particular threat to be documented in a consistent approach. If a context is used to document indicators in a specific way using common terminology, it becomes considerably easy to share this information among the team of individuals working on the issue.

Secondly, IOCs provide security workforce with a set of information that can be fed to automation. Given a set of IOCs for a specific threat, it is possible to scan through an environment to examine if any of them exists on the systems in questions. IOCs can potentially provide a swifter route to instigate detection for new or zero-day attacks for which signatures or detection rules are yet to be developed.

Key Indicators of Compromise

There are several indicators of compromise that an organization should monitor. Below are some of the key

IOCs to keep track of.

1. Unusual Outbound Network Traffic

Unusual traffic Patterns leaving your network perimeter should always be inspected as it is one of the biggest prognostic signs that reveal something is amiss. A common misconception is the assertion that traffic inside the network is secure. Considering that the opportunities of keeping an attacker out of a network is problematic in the face of modern attacks, outbound indicators may be quite easier to monitor.

2. Anomalies In Privileged User Account Activity

Attackers often try to exacerbate privileges of a user account they've hacked. Monitoring privileged accounts for strange activity not only opens a window on possible insider attacks but also unveil accounts that have been taken over by illegal sources. Keeping an eye on systems accessed, time of the activity, type and the volume of data accessed can give early warnings of a possible breach.

3. Geographical Irregularities

Anomalies in login patterns can provide possible evidence of compromise. Connections to locations where your organization normally does not do business might reveal that your sensitive data is being stolen. Accounts noted as logging in from multiple IP addresses in a short period of time combined with location tagging can deliver enough evidence to have a deeper look at that activity.

4. Other Login Red Flags

Excessive failed login attempts on accounts that don't exist provide good evidence that an attacker is trying to get credentials. Similarly, login attempts with usernames of employees who normally wouldn't be working after hours proofs that it isn't really an employee who is accessing data. That might be an attacker at work, not the employee; and it's a red flag for investigation.

5. Surges in Database Read Volume

If an attacker breaches your database storage and seeks to exfiltrate information, there will be signs demonstrating that someone has been mucking about data stores. The exfiltration of any data, especially credit card tables, will generate an enormous amount of read volume which will be way higher than you would normally see on the credit card tables.

6. Large HTML Response Sizes

An attacker using a SQL injection attack against your database will usually have a larger HTML response size than a normal request. For instance, a 30 MB response to a query that is normally around 300 KB can specify that the attacker has successfully implemented a SQL injection attack and dumped the entire user account table or credit card.

7. Large Numbers of Requests for the Same File

When an attacker finds a worthy target on your network, for instance a susceptible web application written in PHP, then manifold attack strings will be executed focusing on that particular file.

8. Mismatched Port-Application Traffic

Attackers often take more advantage of obscure ports to get hold of simple Web filtering techniques. Communications on non-standard ports could be a sign of foul play involving command and control traffic camouflaging as "normal" application behavior.

9. Suspicious Registry Changes

Malware often persists across system reboots by altering the registry to store operational data or to launch a start-up process. Creating a baseline is the vital part when dealing with registry-based IOCs. So make sure to create a clean baseline registry snapshot and look for changes that deviate outside the bounds of the clean 'template'.

10. DNS Request Anomalies

A large prong in DNS (Domain Name Service) requests from a particular host can specify possible malicious activities. Watch out for patterns of DNS requests to external hosts, compare them against geographical region and host repute data. Sifting solutions that are tangled to Threat Intelligence tools can help detect and alleviate malware.

11. Unexpected Patching of Systems

Patching systems is one of the most common transactions that can occur on a network, but if a system is inexplicably patched without any reason, that could indicate a sign of malicious activity. When attackers compromise a system, they want to ensure no other group compromises it, so they patch and strengthen it to prevent other attackers' access.

12. Mobile Device Profile Changes

Since attackers migrate to mobile platforms, organizations should keep an eye on unusual variations to mobile users' device settings. If a mobile device gains a different configuration profile that was not provided by the organization, this may signify a compromise of the user's device and their enterprise credentials. These antagonistic profiles can be installed on a device through a spear-phishing or phishing attack.

13. Bundles of Data in the Wrong Places

In many cases, attackers aggregate data at collection points in a system before endeavoring exfiltration. They try to hide it in unusual locations, such as the directories on Linux machines or root directory of the recycle bin on a Windows-based server that contains temporary files or cached data.

14. Web Traffic with Superhuman Behavior

Infected Computers compromised by a number of click-fraud malware campaigns can generate high volumes of web traffic faster than users sitting at a browser possibly could. In corporate networks, where the users are entitled to use a prescribed browser, monitoring for user agent strings that don't match the internal command can help detect malicious web traffic.

15. Signs of DDoS Activity

Distributed denial-of-service attacks (DDoS) are most frequently used as smokescreens to masquerade other pernicious attacks. If an organization experiences signs of DDoS, such as unavailability of websites, firewall failover, slow network performance, or back-end systems working at utmost capacity for unknown reasons, they shouldn't worry about those immediate snags. It is common for DDoS attacks to engulf security reporting systems, such as SIEM or IPS/IDS solutions. Thus, any DDoS attack should be reviewed for related data breach activity.

The Art of IOC Authoring

With creativity in mind, one can practice generating IOCs. The best Indicators of Compromise have the following properties:

- The IOC detects only the specific attacker activity that has been occurred owing to its suspicious nature. For instance, Monitor for a specific entity in memory (process info, running service info) or look for a set of entries or a specific entry in the Windows Registry. Using these approaches in various combinations provide better matching ability and lessens false positives.

- The IOC is simple and assesses data that is both easy to collect and evaluate.

- The Indicators of Compromise is quite challenging for the attacker to evade without changing tools, tactics or approach methodology.

Tools for Working with IOCs

There are a number of great tools available for working with IOCs, the majority of which are free to use, and all can be tremendously helpful in hunting evil within an organization. To mention just a few:

IOC-EDT

IOC-EDT is a web-based tool used for creating and editing IOC files. Being web based, it enjoys the benefit of being easy to access and use, without the need of installation.

IOC Editor

IOC Editor is a Windows-only GUI (Graphical User Interface) tool that can create a difference between two IOC files, import existing files and build IOCs from scratch.

IOC Finder

IOC Finder is a command line tool that executes scans against a system based off of IOC files. This tool has the benefit of being simple to run from command line.

Therefore, Indicators of compromise are a significant component in the battle against cyber-attacks and malware attacks. Organizations that monitor for IOCs meticulously and keep up with the pioneering IOC discoveries can improve response times and detection rates more significantly.

Module 8
CTI – Adoption and Users

Key Characteristics of CTIs

The complex and evolving landscape of cybercrime introduces your enterprise to new threats on a daily basis. Protecting your corporate assets against cyber-attacks requires a blend of sophisticated technology, expert strategy and an accurate Threat Intelligence data. To combat this new era of threats and software vulnerabilities, more security vendors and enterprises are turning to Cyber Threat Intelligence to stay ahead of today's advanced malware.

Threat Intelligence has become a 'must-have' for organizations when it comes to protecting against cyber-attacks. Threat Intelligence plays a crucial role in protecting the critical resources while empowering businesses. An effective CTI strategy can upsurge the return on security investments and reduce the risks to the organization's assets. However, jotted down are the key characteristics of CTIs.

A Source of Enhanced Threat Intelligence

Cyber security professionals evaluate the quality and efficacy of disparate open source and commercial Threat Intelligence and then analyse it. Unfortunately, many of the indicators they supply are inconsequential or represent threats that are serious for some organizations but can safely be ignored by others. Thus, there is always a need for a Threat Intelligence service that supplies not just threat indicators, but also offers extensive context and malware analysis. This should cover extensive background on threat actors and attack methods linked to threat artifacts or specific indicators.

The Ability to Customize and Prioritize Alerts

Most of the security teams have resources to inspect only a small fraction of alerts they receive from SIEMs and other monitoring systems. This makes it significant to prioritize alerts effectively. The service should include a Threat Intelligence dashboard that informs you about the malware archives and threat indicators that appear most frequently on your network.

Provide Insights into an Active Campaign

Most enterprises already possess abundance of raw information about software vulnerabilities, threats and exploits. However, what organizations need is an insight into active attack campaigns i.e., information that includes the "who, where, when and how" of the most recent security threats. The most valuable insight into active malware campaigns is the information that is specifically relevant to the business context and organization's environment.

Process Oriented

Effective use of Threat Intelligence requires a process oriented approach. Since every organization's environment, business processes and risk tolerance differ, so will their use of Threat Intelligence to inform decisions on these matters. For this reason, the practice of applying external Threat Intelligence has to involve refinement to make it fit into your own set of procedures. Most of the organizations never think systematically about what intelligence is required, what sources are exactly available, or how to gather information to make it readily usable by different audiences.

A well-planned and executed Threat Intelligence program has the potential to provide colossal benefits to your organization. From espionage, to law enforcement, to competitive analysis, all effective intelligence programs follow the same basic process mentioned below:

- Planning and developing intelligence requirements
- Collection of information
- Processing
- Data Analysis and Production
- Dissemination and Integration

Adversary Based

Threat Intelligence activities are organized around specific adversaries, especially cybercriminals, hacktivists and cyber-espionage agents. The organization that knows its opponents can amplify its defenses to protect against those adversaries and the attacks they implement. The intelligence gathered will be used to inform decision makers regarding adversary tools, tactics, and procedures.

Provide Insights Relevant to Risk

Threat Intelligence programs are usually based on the evaluation of information assets that the organization needs to protect. These assets include documents, data & intellectual property such as engineering drawings and customer databases, and computing resources such as websites, source code, applications and networks. Threat Intelligence may provide a deep insight into the likelihood of risk and its impact on the business.

Create New Protections and Prevent Future Attacks

Many people envisage Threat Intelligence services in terms of analyzing and prioritizing threats. But the competencies to create new protections and prevent forthcoming attacks can pay major outcomes. When you discover new kinds of malware or threat artifacts, you should be able to create custom tags and have to share those tags and artifacts with other organizations. This will allow you to identify relevant threat indicators before they hit your network.

In an environment with tight budgets, the

implementation of a Cyber Threat Intelligence program using a phased and requirements-based approach can materially enhance the overall security posture of the organization.

Cyber Threat Intelligence is rapidly becoming an ever-higher business priority. The growth and sophistication of cyber-attacks against individuals and enterprises have made traditional cyber security measures virtually archaic. The term "Threat Intelligence" swiftly emerged onto the information security landscape over the last few years, and many security vendors now offer Threat Intelligence services to customers.

Cyber Threat Intelligence (CTI) is an ecosystem that supports the decision-making process resulting from the data collection, Processing, analysis, dissemination and integration of threats and vulnerabilities to an organization and its people and assets. A well-defined and operationalized CTI solution acts as a purposeful planning tool to support the organization's threat model, business goals and security operations.

In cyber security landscape, intelligence data includes information concerning threats and vulnerabilities, both external and internal to an organization, that are potentially malicious in nature and may result in the compromise of systems or assets, leading to the exfiltration of sensitive data. By receiving routine and time sensitive intelligence information from both indigenous and tangentially deployed collection elements, organizations can cross-cue among internal intelligence collectors, briskly propagating plans of action to satisfy all levels of requirements.

Cyber Threat Sharing

Sharing Threat Intelligence is not a common practice, but it can serve as the most valuable asset in the battle against malicious cyber-attacks. The intricacy of hackers has reached a point where it is no longer about keeping them out of the network, but confining their activity once they are inside. Understanding the prominence of Threat Intelligence sharing is the first step in building a strong stratagem against malicious outsiders.

By sharing Threat Intelligence, one can avoid major security incidents from recurring and thwart emerging threats from claiming more victims. Threat Intelligence sharing has boomed in prominence, giving birth to initiatives such as the Cyber Threat Alliance, an agglomeration of security solution vendors and researchers who have joined forces to mutually share information and protect their customers.

The evolution of Threat Intelligence sharing is culminating, with the development of platforms and standards that allow organizations gather, organize, share and identify sources of Threat Intelligence. However, benefits of sharing threat information include:

Shared Situational Awareness

Threat Intelligence sharing enables organizations to leverage the collective knowledge, experiences, and methodology of their sharing partners, thereby enhancing the defensive capabilities of both organizations.

Improved Decision Making

Threat Intelligence sharing enables entities to make superior decisions with promptness and self-assurance.

In-Depth Understanding of Cyber Threats

Threat Intelligence sharing allows organizations to develop and share intelligence, which helps them improve their understanding of the threat environment and offer them the capability to customize and deploy security controls, countermeasures, corrective actions and detection methods based on discovered changes in the threat environment.

Despite of many benefits of Threat Intelligence sharing, covered organizations and business associates face certain challenges as well. To mention few:

Protecting Privacy

Although many organizations may be able to participate in Threat Intelligence-sharing program, some are still required to anonymize their contributions.

Risk of Disclosing Sensitive Data

Disclosing sensitive data, such as PII, PHI, trade secrets, intellectual property or other proprietary information can result in huge financial losses, violations of sharing agreements or federal regulations, legal action and loss of repute.

Legal and Organization Restrictions

An organization's legal and executive teams may restrict on the types of data that the organization can share. Restrictions may include limits on the types of data as well as the level of technical detail provided.

Cyber Warfare

The digital world has brought about a new type of clear and contemporary danger - Cyberwar. Since information technology and the internet have advanced to such a great extent, cyber war has become the drumbeat of the day as nation-states are mobilizing themselves for the cyber battlespace.

Cyber warfare is an Internet-based conflict involving politically driven attacks on information and information systems. To sum up, it involves the actions by a nation-state or international organization to attack and endeavour to damage another nation's computers or information networks through, for example, denial-of-service attacks or computer viruses. Cyber warfare attacks can interrupt or disable essential services, disable official websites and networks, alter or steal classified data, and paralyze financial systems - among many other possibilities.

The most effectual protection against cyber warfare attacks is securing information and networks. Security updates need to be applied to all systems including those that are not considered perilous because any susceptible system can be co-opted and used to carry out attacks. Measures to alleviate the potential damage of an attack include wide disaster recovery planning that further includes provisions for extended outages.

Types of Cyber-Warfare attacks
There are several different types of cyber-warfare, from specialized hacking jobs on a specific server to generally-targeted denial of service attacks. They include the following:

Vandalism
Cyber vandalism is a common terminology for hackers who use illegal digital tools in pursuit of political ends. Hacktivists cause mutilation through virtual modification or destruction of content by hacking websites and disabling or disrupting servers by data overload. Some even conduct cyber operations on behalf of personal political causes such as the human rights, environment and animal rights. Cyber vandalism, sometimes also called 'cyber hacktivism,' is the most widespread form of cyber war and garners a great deal of public attention.

Denial of Service

Denial of Service (DoS) refers to an attack that engulfs a system with data - usually a flood of simultaneous requests sent to a website to monitor its pages, causing the web server to crash or simply become defective as it struggles to respond to more requests than it can handle. The DoS attack is one of the most common attacks on the Internet.

Cyber espionage

Cyber espionage is an act or practice of obtaining secrets from individuals, rivals, groups, competitors, governments and enemies for political, military or economic advantage using illegal exploitation methods on networks, internet, software and/or computers. It consists of the search for access to personal or corporate data, intellectual property, proprietary rights and information, or outcomes from research and development projects, etc.

Cyber Threat Intelligence Requirements

The increasing volume and speed of vibrant and emerging threats has left organizations clambering to effectively respond. By incorporating Cyber Threat Intelligence (CTI) into security operations, leading organizations can curtail the time to detection of relevant threats and respond more efficiently. Effectual counterintelligence provides the organizations with the necessary information required to enhance defense-in-depth.

Setting up the requirements is the first task to be accomplished before investing time in collecting and researching any type of intelligence. By aggregating and analyzing threat data comprising adversary profiles and correlated tools, tactics, and procedures (TTPs), it is possible to detect and track specific attack groups, correlate tactical stages and integrate private and open source information to counteract the adversary TTPs.

Developing a requirements-based model plays a vital role in driving the success of a CTI program. Therefore, a proper model has to define the requirements and also its priority, in order to ensure that the most critical and most relevant information is processed and not lost in the noise. An effective Threat Intelligence programme will have a number of areas of focus. Organizations that employ Cyber-Threat Intelligence model must rely profoundly on analyzing and consuming CTI information with an ardent decision maker influencing its risk management.

Requirement gathering is a step that is often overlooked and is also the key to an efficacious programme. Developing a good set of requirements helps the security organizations to:

- Invigilate the right threat actors
- Accumulate the most useful intelligence

- Avoid wasting money and time collecting and disseminating trifling data
- Prepare intelligence in the correct format and level of detail for each type of user

The goal of a Cyber Threat Intelligence requirement is to define what data an analyst needs to collect in order to fill a knowledge gap. It is quite imperative to define the requirement as sternly as possible so that the analyst does not waste resources and time collecting unnecessary or conflicting information. This also simultaneously helps the analyst to determine which collection sources are the best to gain information from. Requirements break down into three categories:

Intelligence Requirements

A common question that Threat Intelligence professional's encounter is whether their organization's intelligence requirements should be adversary focused or attack surface based. Basically, intelligence requirements comprise knowns and unknowns that revolve around questions that the intelligence function needs to answer to provide judgment-based, knowledge-backed decisions. This provides a great advantage as it supports decisions with empirical data.

Collection Requirements

Collection requirements can either be externally focused or internally focused. Externally focused collection requirements include requirements that are adversary/cyber threat actor focused whereas internally focused collection requirements entail visibility on the subject organization's attack surface.

Production requirements

The production requirements should be comprehensive enough to encompass short-term requirements that instantly head to the top of the priority list. Production requirements allow the intelligence function to have a well-defined template and cadence for the intelligence product output.

Other Key CTI Requirements:
Assets That Must Be Prioritized

Personal Information

Personally identifiable information (PII) or Sensitive personal information (SPI) includes names, birthdays, addresses, medical records, Social Security and national identification numbers. PII can be employed in mass phishing attacks, vended on concealed websites, and can be used to create fake accounts that attackers can monetize. Cybercriminals and hackers can also use it as the source for spear phishing attacks against target enterprises.

Credit Card and Financial Account Data

Bank account numbers, credit card numbers and account access credentials are tremendously valuable to cybercriminals as they can be sold in bulk on underground websites. The costs of losing such sensitive data are extremely high as it includes data breach notification charges, expenses to offer customers with credit monitoring facilities, legal fees, and regulatory fines.

Intellectual Property

Intellectual property (IP) includes software programs, engineering designs, technical documents, product manuals and innovative works such as music recordings, videos and books. Theft of Intellectual property consigned to you by someone else can lead to violations of license agreements and contractual obligations.

Confidential Business Information

Confidential business information encompasses business plans, competitive bid information, customer lists and trade secrets. Confidential business data also includes information on financial results, amalgamation, and other news that affects stock prices. The leak of confidential emails, memos and draft press releases can prove costly to stakeholders, and even elicit criminal investigations.

Credentials and IT Systems Information

IT systems information and Login credentials can be extremely valuable to adversaries, possibly opening the way for the huge loss of every kind of information asset in the enterprises. Thus, ensure that service providers, suppliers and other third parties with access to your systems are assiduous in protecting the login credentials for your systems.

Intelligence Consumers

To develop CTI requirements, one must understand the prerequisites of the people and systems using the intelligence. Those needs include the information content that people require to do their works and the formats that make data accessible to people and security systems. However, let's have a look at some of these requirements, which include

Tactical users

Network operations center (NOC) staff members need legitimate malware signatures and URL reputations to allow malware gateways, firewalls, IDS/IPS systems, and other gateway security products to stop attacks without blocking legal traffic or producing false positives. On the other hand, SOC analysts monitor alerts and decide on the ones that have to be escalated for further analysis. For this purpose, they require accurate, relevant, and timely data fed to quickly decide which ones are isolated events and which ones might be part of multifaceted attacks.

Operational users

Operational users of intelligence, such as forensic analysts, fraud detection departments and IR teams, need detailed context around events and alerts. They also need in-depth intelligence on attacks and adversaries to quickly determine which systems have been compromised and which systems need to be remediated. The types of intelligence they require for these activities include breakdowns of targeted attacks, analyses of malware and reports on the tactics, techniques, and procedures (TTPs) of specific adversaries or attacks.

Strategic users

Strategic users, including IT managers and CISOs, need CTI reports that enable them to understand trends and make superior decisions about process improvements, new technologies, security budgets and staffing levels. Good intelligence helps them curtail risks and defend new business and technology initiatives.

Cyber Threat Intelligence is rapidly moving from an over-used industry buzzword, to being recognized as a necessity for organizations to understand and stay ahead of swiftly evolving threats. Security organizations are also investing in better ways to detect, prevent and respond to attacks. The incorporation of Threat Intelligence into a security strategy and tactical operations plan needs forethought, supervision and goals aligned with business requirements.

In the current cybersecurity landscape, it is unfeasible to prevent all breaches or attacks. Traditional cybersecurity defenses are becoming ineffectual and organizations are struggling to cope. Thereofore, organizations must counter the attackers with sophisticated measures, but most are only able to respond to the attacks they can detect, and are progressively confused about how they can make the significant developments needed.

Cyber Threat Intelligence (CTI) is an advanced process that enables enterprises to incessantly gather valuable insights based on the scrutiny of contextual and situational risks and customize it according to the organization's specific threat landscape, its industry and markets. Threat Intelligence complements fundamentally reactive network defense tactics with a proactive approach that alleviates threats more effectually and intelligently by driving out malicious actors away from an organization's perimeter.

The purpose of Threat Intelligence is to identify, acknowledge, handle and alleviate advanced persistent threats (APT). This intelligence can create a huge difference in proactively reacting to cyber-attacks before they even occur. Cyber Threat Intelligence is all about employing cyber-attack events, understanding the core environment and pinpointing potential targets of the hackers.

In this threat landscape, the use of CTI is becoming more imperative to IT security and response teams than ever before. CTI is beneficial because it focuses on the primary concern of the business, by enhancing cyber defenses and reducing cyber risks. The factors that need to be considered to make Threat Intelligence really useful include accuracy, timeliness, actionability, and relevance.

Some of the key benefits of implementing CTI are:

- Improved visibility into threats

- Better and more informed decisions
- Reduced actual exposure of sensitive data & business outages
- Faster and more precise response
- Reduced number of incidents through more intelligent blocking

Acquiring and Using CTI

Since the intelligence security teams have become more comfortable with leveraging CTI data, they are persistently seeking new and varied sources of CTI. Currently, majority of security teams using Cyber Threat Intelligence are acquiring this information from community sharing groups and industry, and are using commercial feeds from security intelligence vendors. Reutilizing threat data gathered from internal processes can be viewed as a sign of maturing organizations.

Vendor-Provided CTI

Security teams purchase or acquire CTI from different types of vendors such as Endpoint security vendors, unified threat management (UTM)/firewall/IDS vendors, CTI platform vendors, vulnerability management providers, SIEM vendors, application security vendors and a variety of others.

Network and host-based security vendors that regularly witness malicious network traffic patterns and signatures, malware samples, and real attacks emanating from certain systems and subnets are in a better position to provide tactical data than other vendors. Vulnerability management vendors have real-time experience with malware, vulnerabilities and exploits in applications and systems, which can also provide highly useful information. Thus, it would be interesting to witness how the applications of CTI services and dedicated CTI platforms changes over time in comparison.

Top Use Cases for CTI

An increasing number of CISOs (chief information security officers) are currently realizing the value of Threat Intelligence to protecting organizations against cybercrimes. However, the top three use cases for CTI data are:

- Blocking malicious IP addresses or domains at egress points (for example: firewalls)

- Examining DNS server logs for malicious IP addresses or domains

- Adding context to investigations or compromise assessments

Consumers of CTI

The two top consumers of Cyber Threat Intelligence are the security operations center (SOC), the primary consumer and incident responders, the big consumer. Most of the CTI programs seek to advance and enable detection and response activities; however, these are the primary teams involved in most cases.

Improving Detection and Response

As the attacker landscape has become more sophisticated than ever, understanding the malware tactics is quite vital. With this improved visibility and context, respondents must be able to respond more quickly to incidents.

With CTI, defenders can avail some insight into the types of malware, local exploits, network traffic patterns, delivery mechanisms and overall attack strategies that other organizations are viewing in the wild. For this reason, visibility into attacker tactics and strategy is considered to be the most valuable benefit of CTI. With sound CTI informations, security teams can readily look for patterns and indicators of malicious activity, and thus respond more rapidly. Over time, this will normally lead to fewer incidents or more consistent approaches to incident detection and analysis in organizations environments.

Integrating CTI Feeds

Currently, organizations are integrating many tools into their CTI feed information, including their application security, edge and host security, identity and access management (IAM) systems, and vulnerability management systems. Most of the security teams implement CTI into detection tools than into response tools. For detection, the top tools for integration include vulnerability management, firewalls, SIEM and UTM platforms. For response tool integration, only vulnerability management and forensic analysis tools make a significant contribution in terms of integration. All of these tools allow for both detection and quarantining/blocking of threats, which supports well with the purpose of integrating CTI.

Generally, organizations find numerous ways to integrate CTI data feeds into these defense and response systems. For example, usage of prebuilt connectors from vendors, utilization of custom APIs, vendor-provided APIs and API development kits, and engaging the services of intelligence service providers and third-party integrators.

The importance of CTI seems to be an inevitable conclusion. The knowledge, tools, tactics and processes around the practical implementation of CTI are maturing, but they need to mature more rapidly in order for organizations to detect, investigate and block threats as needed. Currently, there is an enormous amount of confusion and dissonance in the CTI marketplace. A major source of burden for many security professionals is the unduly general nature of many CTI feeds. Therefore, the process of CTI collection, consumption and utilization need to be enhanced as CTI implementation grows and becomes more systematic in organizations.

Though some organizations may not require Cyber Threat Intelligence, it is still recommended by the researchers to try and implement it for a specific period of time just to deduct if the organization is vulnerable to cyber-attacks and advanced persistent threats (APT). CTI implementation is the only way to determine if the organization is susceptible to any threats at all. Any information about the trend of attacks occurring to the organization's network is beneficial because this will pre-determine the necessary actions.

Thus, Integrating Cyber Threat Intelligence into enterprises cybersecurity stratagems can enable decision-makers at all phases to better understand the nature of the threats they face and also to pursue the organization's strategic security goals more efficiently.

Module 9
Cyber Kill Chain

Cyber Kill Chain

As attacks have become more sophisticated, the concept of Cyber Kill Chain has become common in security discussions. This approach is based on the premise that attacks have an operational life cycle to collect information.

Lockheed Martin developed the Cyber Kill Chain to describe the different stages of an attack from initial reconnaissance to objective completion. The better security professionals understand the kill chain life cycle, the more chances they have to intrude, manipulate and even prevent the attack from succeeding. The 7 stages of the Cyber Kill Chain increase visibility into an attack and enhance an analyst's understanding of an adversary's TTPs.

Seven Phases of Cyber Kill Chain

1. Reconnaissance

During reconnaissance, an intruder is seeking information that might disclose vulnerabilities and weak points in the target network or systems. Reconnaissance tools also include technical tactics such as scanning ports for vulnerabilities, services and applications to exploit.

2. Weaponization

This is an essential phase for defenders to understand. In this stage, adversaries analyse the data collected on their targets to determine what attack techniques to use. Intruders create remote access malware weapon, such as a worm or virus, tailored to one or more vulnerabilities. Attackers may even target specific operating systems, firewalls and other technologies.

3. Delivery

This is the most important opportunity for defenders to block the operation. At this step, the weapon is transmitted to the victim, via e-mail attachments, websites or USB drives. A key measure of efficacy is the fraction of intrusion attempts that are blocked at delivery stage.

4. Exploitation

Once after the weapon is delivered to the victim, the exploitation stage triggers the attackers exploit. Generally, the exploitation targets an operating system or application vulnerability. Here, traditional hardening measures add flexibility, but custom capabilities are necessary to stop zero-day exploits at this stage.

5. Installation

At this phase, the weapon is installed to either attack the computer or install a remote "backdoor" so that the intruder can access the system. Therefore, analyze installation phase during malware scrutiny to create new endpoint mitigations.

6. Command & Control

The defender's last best chance to block the operation

is by blocking the Command & control channel. To communicate and pass information to and fro, attackers set up command and control channels to operate between infected devices and themselves. If attackers can't issue commands, defenders can prevent impact.

7. Actions on Objectives

The longer an adversary has Command and Control access, the greater the impact. Intruders take action to achieve their goals such as data destruction, data exfiltration or encryption for ransom. Defenders must detect this phase as swiftly as possible by using forensic evidence – including network packet captures, for damage appraisal.

Cyber kill chain is structured to divulge the active state of a data breach. With a solid security-in-depth strategy, coupled with right tools and people, organizations can prevent and stop on-going attacks before the damage is done.

Tactical, Operational & Strategic Cyber Intelligence

Cyber Threat Intelligence is an analytical discipline that requires a clear understanding of the values and elements on all three Threat Intelligence levels, namely: tactical, operational and strategic. These three levels of intelligence in cyberspace are used to protect vulnerable infrastructure, thwart off attacks and prevent known and unknown threats.

Tactical Threat Intelligence

Tactical Cyber Threat Intelligence is one of the most useful forms of intelligence in terms of protecting the organisation against malware attacks. Conversely, tactical Threat Intelligence is used to monitor threat actors to help predict attacks through their procedures and techniques.

Tactical intelligence informs what an organization needs to focus on while responding to incidents employing the tools at their disposal. This encompasses indicators such as IP addresses, domains and hashes that an organization is most likely to encounter. Tactical intelligence is much more temporal in nature than strategic intelligence and the utility of it can dispel quickly. The tactical phase of the cyber domain is where on-the-network actions take place. And this is where network defenders and malevolent actors maneuver against each other.

Operational Threat Intelligence

Operational Threat Intelligence is litigable information on specific incoming attacks. Ideally, it apprises on the nature of the attack, the capability and identity of the attacker – and gives an indication of when the attack is likely to take place. It is used to alleviate the attack: for example, by hardening services or removing attack paths. Usually, operational Threat Intelligence is utilized when actionable intelligence of a pending attack on an industry or customer is discovered.

The operational level is where a hacktivist group may plan both physical and cyber world activities to support their objectives. Operational level analysts should always attempt to serve as the bridge between the tactical level analysts and the strategic level players.

Some examples of operational level intelligence are:

- Revelation of adversary tools, tactics and procedures.
- Clear understanding of the adversary operational cycle
- Technical, social, financial, legal or other vulnerabilities that the adversary has.
- Information that allows the defender to influence an adversary as they move through the kill chain.

Strategic Threat Intelligence

Strategic Threat Intelligence is utilized by high-level strategists within an organisation, usually the board or those who report to the board. Its main intention is to help strategists understand current risks, and to identify further risks that an organization is unaware of. Generally, it deals with high-level concepts such as risk and likelihoods, rather than technical aspects.

To sum up, strategic Threat Intelligence informs

how an organization defends itself and its overall cyber security posture. This comprises the tools necessary to defend against the threats' capabilities. Employing strategic Threat Intelligence allows an organization to tactically respond when issues or incidents arise.

Some examples of Strategic Threat Intelligence might include:

- Indications that a foreign government or competitor may have previously acquired intellectual property (IP) via cyber exploitation.
- Decision by a competitor or a potential competitor to enter market space

Understanding the levels of Cyber Threat Intelligence, and their utilities can significantly augment an organization's capability to leverage Threat Intelligence and respond to intelligence requirements more efficiently.

The Intelligence Cycle

The Intelligence Cycle is a process of developing raw data into finished intelligence for policymakers to employ in decision making and action. It is a continuous process conducted by intelligence teams to provide guidance with relevant and timely intelligence to mitigate risks and uncertainty. Throughout the intelligence cycle, teams require evaluation and feedback from management.

To better understand intelligence and its cycle, it is significant to know the clear and critical distinction between intelligence and information. Information refers to data that has been congregated, but not further developed through analysis, interpretation, or correlation with other intelligence or data. The application of analysis transmutes information into intelligence. Both information and intelligence are imperative, and both may exist together in some form. They are not the same but have different applicability, connotations and creditability.

Here are the five steps that constitute the Intelligence Cycle:

Direction
Planning and direction for information gathering includes management of the entire intelligence effort, from priority intelligence requirements to delivering the final intelligence product.

Collection
Following the entrenched direction, the Threat Intelligence service potentially collects useful raw data from relevant sources to produce finished intelligence.

Processing
The collected data is amalgamated into a standardized format pertinent for detailed analysis. It involves converting the vast amount of data collected to a form usable by analysts through language translations,

decryption and data reduction.

Analysis

The gathered data is scrutinized by subject matter specialists to identify potential threats to customer environments. Countermeasures to respond to detected threats may also be developed in this phase.

Dissemination

In this step, the intelligence analysis is distributed to consumers so that appropriate defensive measures can be taken.

At the highest level, the Threat Intelligence cycle follows the classic computing procedure model of input-process-output. Most Cyber Threat Intelligence functions have espoused this basic model and, while the terms for the three phases may vary, the most widely used ones are collection-analysis-dissemination. Some Threat Intelligence functions prefer to conclude the cycle with a review activity that leads to an adjustment in future. In this way, the intelligence function can match the pace of change in both intelligence field and threat environment.

The intelligence life cycle will now be considered in detail.

Direction

The intelligence cycle usually begins with direction from the customer, who is an appropriate representative of the body of people utilizing the intelligence product. In this phase, the requirements and priorities are set. It is the springboard from which all Intelligence Cycle activities are launched and is the base for the entire process.

This part of the process includes determining the data requirement, deciding how to collect that data, and setting up an agenda for collecting the information. Usually, in such cases, the consumers have a requirement for a specific intelligence product. That product might be a graphic image, a full report or raw information that is accumulated, processed, and disseminated, but skips the analysis and production step.

If intelligence holdings can deliver the required information, the collection, processing, analysis and production phases are by-passed, and the intelligence is dispersed. If the requirement cannot be fulfilled from current intelligence holdings, suitable command, direction and action are essential to identify collection requirements and task collection resources.

Planning and Direction Phase Synchronizing Phases

Effectual management and guidance are necessary to ensure clear and precise communication between intelligence activities and to organize the various phases within the cycle. Responsibility for the overall management and supervision of the intelligence life cycle begins in the direction phase.

Determining Requirements

The initial stage in the intelligence cycle and the dynamic force behind the work one do is the identification of specific user requirements. If you are a producer of intelligence, then those specified intelligence requirements must serve as a road map or guide to focus your exertions in the proper direction. If you are a user of intelligence, make sure the intelligence requirements you develop exactly state the problem you deal with.

The customer's intelligence requirements typically divide into three directives:

- Long-term directives that set the wide scope which normally persists for 1–2 years

- Short-term directives that are tactical and narrow in scope and are usually handled within days.

- Medium-term directives are oriented towards a specific topic which is normally handled within weeks or months.

Standing and Specific Requirements

Direction is imperative because it provides the

intelligence analyst a start point. Each intelligence organisation will have their unique information requirements. However, direction will come in the form of either 'specific information requirements' or 'standing information requirements'.

Standing Information Requirements

Standing requirements are usually tied to the organizational mission and don't change often. Sometimes referred to as Enduring Intelligence Requirements, they provide information necessary for mid and long-range planning. Standing requirements are broad, continuing requirements that generally follow a fixed pattern.

Specific Information Requirements

Specific information requirements emanate from the necessity to know a particular piece of information. Also referred as 'Requests for Information (RFIs)', they are used to inform a plan or deliberate an action. Therefore, the effective planning and direction of the intelligence effort involve a clear understanding of the needs of a variety of consumers.

Collection

The second phase includes all those activities that involve the collection of information to satisfy the requirements that were defined. Data collection is usually performed through five basic intelligence sources: Geospatial Intelligence (GEOINT), Measurement and

Signature Intelligence (MASINT), Human Intelligence (HUMINT), Open-Source Intelligence (OSINT), and Signals Intelligence (SIGINT).

The data collection can be done either via human or technical means and involves gathering information from a variety of sources. The purpose of this collection is to meet the defined strategic or tactical goals. Data collection usually consumes the greatest amount of budget because of the effort, time and cost involved in collecting information from diverse sources. To ensure effectual and economical use of collection resources, collection activities should accomplish the following guidelines:

- Accurately determine the value of collected data.

- Plan randomly so that the attackers cannot determine a pattern and evade coverage.

- Swiftly and accurately distribute critical and perishable data.

- Be systematic to minimize missed opportunities.

- Be synchronized to promote natural assistance, reduce duplication and spread the knowledge of imposed techniques.

Collection strategy

Constant monitoring of every possible piece of data to a high degree of detail is not technically feasible. Therefore, an intelligence function needs to shape its collection strategy according to the following considerations: Firstly, breadth vs depth. In most cases, finding the data or information is not the issue. The hardest part lies in filtering out that data which is relevant to the analysis task. Therefore, a careful balance has to be made between 'detailed but narrow' or 'broad but shallow'.

Secondly, monitor frequency. Monitoring is a cyclical process driven by a pulse. The pulse should be sufficiently long such that monitored organization does not incur unnecessary computational expense or cause undue delay. Conversely, it should be sufficiently short such that it does not deteriorate beyond correction between pulses. Therefore, monitoring frequency will be one or a combination of the following.

- Periodic monitoring – Inspecting the environment at a regular frequency which might range from minutes to months or more.

- Event-driven monitoring – Inspecting the environment in an ad-hoc method that is driven by specific events occurring, or expected to occur, within the threat landscape.

- Analysis-driven monitoring - Monitoring

or inspecting the environment in an ad-hoc manner which is determined by the current state of the analysis.

Each of these aspects has its own advantages and disadvantages. The main aim is to ensure maximum effectiveness of the analysis given to the customer's needs and characteristics of the cyber threat.

Standard Technical Reports Using Modules

Collection can be further enriched by launching a Standard Technical Report Using Modules (STRUM) that enables auto entity extraction at the point of data collection and analysis. Inducing this methodology to Cyber Threat Intelligence and other security applications is considered a keystone of Cyber Threat Intelligence capability development.

STRUM facilitates technical interoperability amid sectors and information sharing forums. Cataloguing also enables security managers to envisage the threat spectrum more systematically than current practices of swapping cyber network attack experiences informally. Currently, there are number of established STRUM formats operating within the cyber security landscape.

Processing

The processing step involves the use of specialized,

highly trained personnel and technologically sophisticated equipment to convert the raw data into understandable and usable information. For instance, the processing step comprises entry of data into a computer, collation of paper files, reduction of data and other forms of information management. Effectual processing and collation requires a clear understanding of the collection plan, consumers' needs, analytic strategy and the types of information that are being processed.

Processing is a critical and often-overlooked phase in the Threat Intelligence cycle. Generally, this will involve the applications of automated tools that can perform valuable data processing functions such as parsing, filtering, correlating, de-duplicating and aggregating.

Analysis

During the analysis phase, raw data is transmuted into information in the form of trends, patterns, sequences, clusters and so on. This is attained via a sequence of primitive inferences such as selection, cataloguing, abstraction, specification, assessment, matching, instantiation, correlation and transformation. If the information generated during the analysis phase provides sufficient understanding for alleviating a harmful event, then it can be termed as intelligence.

The analysis comprises of facts, findings and forecasts that define the element of study and allow the assessment and anticipation of events and outcomes. The analysis should be timely, objective and most importantly accurate. To generate intelligence objectively, the analysts apply four basic forms of reasoning - deduction, induction, abduction and the scientific method. The analysis stage also requires well-trained and specialized personnel to give meaning to the processed data and to prioritize it against known requirements.

Analysis is broadly classified into two categories: strategic and tactical intelligence. Tactical intelligence is the output of scrutiny that produces litigable information for immediate operations. On the other hand, strategic intelligence is broader and mainly focuses on strategic priorities.

Situational Awareness & Understanding

Today's leaders need meaningful cyber situational awareness and understanding to safeguard sensitive data, withstand fundamental operations, and defend national infrastructure. Cyber situational awareness brings together all the information that an organization holds about itself, its attack surface, its partners and its threat environment in a form that is customized to that specific organization. This will help organization to understand on how to adapt its security countermeasures in the longer term.

Attaining the level of situational awareness requires an investment in data collection, management, and scrutiny to maintain an on-going picture of how the networks, computer systems, and users are operating in an organization. Comprehensive cyber situation awareness and understanding involves three key areas: Network awareness, Threat/Attack awareness and Operational/ mission awareness

Network Awareness

This usually comprises of clear understanding of the condition and status of the elements that encompass the network. The elements such as servers, power, appliances and cabling are required for the network to function. The network awareness also includes a recovery time, which comprises anything from a reboot, to a patch or to a hardware failure. The process of gaining network awareness is listed below:

- Disciplined asset and configuration management
- Periodic vulnerability auditing
- Patch management and acquiescence reporting
- Identify and share incident awareness across the organizations

Threat/Attack Awareness

Threat Awareness reveals a variety of activities taking place on the network by tracking customers IP addresses and domain names and monitoring. It identifies, appraises and prioritizes risks and potential threats to enable planning, response, countermeasures and remediation. The process of gaining threat awareness is mentioned below:

- Identify and monitor internal incidents and skeptical behaviour
- Incorporate knowledge of external threat
- Participate in cross-government or cross-industry threats-sharing communities on potential indicators and warning.

Operational Awareness

This apprises on how the degraded network operations will affect the mission of the network. With this awareness, negative situations can be identified and managed as and when they occur. The process of gaining operational awareness includes:

- Developing a complete picture of the critical dependencies to operate efficiently in cyber landscape.

- Understanding these acute dependencies to support mission impact in forensic investigation.

Principles of Intelligence

The principle of intelligence refers to the need to obtain accurate information concerning the actions and movements of the attackers. The analysis of processing should be conducted within the established principles of intelligence mentioned below:

❑ **Planning** - Proper planning will ensure that correct information is received at the right time and place. Planning is an action that needs to be considered well before any deliberate action is planned. Planning will also ensure that the intelligence requirements are met.

❑ **Objectivity** - Intelligence must be factual, unbiased, intellectually authentic and free of prejudice.

❑ **Perspective** - Get inside the mind-set of the key actors, especially adversaries and try to think from the attacker's perspective.

❑ **Dexterity** - Dexterity is nothing but an ability to exploit information in context at the accurate tempo. Look ahead, find out threats and opportunities, cultivate the flexibility to respond to fluctuating situations and be prepared to exploit opportunities as they arise.

- ❑ **Timeliness** - Providing intelligence promptly will assist commanders to make better decisions at a pace that upholds the initiative.

- ❑ **Relevancy** - The collection effort must be relevant to the intelligence requirements. This will ensure that time, energy, and resources are not wasted in collecting irrelevant data. Furthermore, irrelevant information and intelligence can mislead planners and strategists.

- ❑ **Exploitation of all Sources** - All overt, discreet, covert and clandestine sources available must be exploited. Additionally, these sources need to be prudently considered in order to prevent one source compromising another.

Suitably Qualified & Experienced Personnel

Intelligence driven threat detection and response enables organizations achieve high standards of security despite today's swiftly escalating and erratic threat environment. In spite of these initiatives, cyber-crime remains a tactical problem for policing due to a variety of factors such as lack of financial resources and capacity as well as suitably qualified and experienced personnel (SQEP). SQEP is a person who has sufficient qualifications and rich experience in a defined skill area, to be able to incorporate that skill at one of the five levels mentioned below:

- Supervised
- Unsupervised
- Advising and guiding others
- Externally recognised "expert"
- Company "expert"

The selection of Suitably Qualified and Experienced Personnel should not be essentially restricted to those with formal training and experience of law enforcement or intelligence. It is considered that the below mentioned skillsets constitute an appropriate blend of skills for a cyber-Threat Intelligence team:

- Fraud Analysis
- Intelligence management and leadership
- Data Science and Statistical Analytics
- Intelligence Investigation
- IT Network Engineering
- Software coder (AV and Malware)

Dissemination

Essentially, this step involves the delivery of the finished product to the consumers who requested the information. Typically, dissemination of the information is achieved through means such as email, websites, and hardcopy distribution. The finished product is usually referred to as "finished intelligence." Recipients of intelligence reports will be placed at tactical, operational and strategic levels inside business functions and technology functions. These recipients of intelligence then take action or make decisions based on the intelligence that has been provided.

The main purpose of dissemination is to ensure that the intelligence product reaches its destination in a timely and credible manner. This phase should also include an opportunity for feedback, to appraise the value of the intelligence that has been delivered. The actions, decisions and feedback may lead to the levying of more information requirements, thereby triggering the intelligence cycle once again.

Dissemination is not a trivial activity. If the consumer is to acquire and benefit from an intelligence product then three vital criteria need to be met:

- The right content - Good quality intelligence must provide sufficient understanding to allow consumers to alleviate a harmful event.

- The right presentation - Intelligence must be concise, accurate, and understandable and strike the right balance between tables, numbers, narrative, graphics and multimedia.

- The right time - Intelligence must be dispersed within a time frame as this allows consumers to make effective and proactive decisions.

The above principles are highly interconnected. The best intelligence in the world will be obsoletely useless if it cannot be understood or reaches too late.

The process of the Threat Intelligence cycle is a base for Intelligence teams to establish their efforts and maintain alignment with stakeholders. With the clear understandings of the fundamentals of Threat Intelligence cycle, one can fully incorporate intelligence into operations. This integration allows intelligence to support both planning and execution efficiently and effectively.

Threats change over time, as do risks. A vibrant Threat Intelligence capability helps to ensure that security operations can also keep pace with those changes. The use of Cyber Threat Intelligence has gained immense popularity as the value of threat prediction and proactive defense building has proven to be effectual in mitigating threat activities. CTI provides information that links the possibility and impact of a cyber-attack by providing a framework for timely investigation and prioritization of potential threats & vulnerabilities in an industry's threat landscape.

Developing a Cyber Threat Intelligence program

brings insight to the specific threats that increase risk in the organization. CTI program allows an organization to strategically prioritize its defense methods to focus efforts on what can cause severe damage to the business. It helps to ensure business stability and, eventually, the success of the organization.

Module 10
Threat Intelligence
Collection and Analysis

Threat Intelligence Platform

As the threat landscape continues to evolve and accelerate, the security industry persists to respond with a range of disparate new detection technologies. Even the most vigorous traditional security cannot effectively defend an organization from today's targeted cyber threats. Only innovative thinking that redefines cyber security strategy can outsmart the threat actors in the cyber war.

Transforming Threat Intelligence data from manifold sources into contextual, actionable information is a challenge that many organizations currently face . Due to the ever-increasing volume of cyber-attacks and regulatory pressures, there is an urgent requirement for a new type of enterprise platform – a platform that can support the whole security team from the chief information security officer (CISO) to the threat-analyst and security teams in the trenches performing daily incident response, threat analysis and network defense.

Threat Intelligence Platform (TIP) is an evolving technology discipline that helps organizations aggregate, correlate, and scrutinize threat data from many sources in real time to support defensive activities. TIPs have emerged to address the escalating amount of data produced by a variety of external and internal resources (such as Threat Intelligence feeds and system logs) and help security teams detect the threats that are pertinent to their organization.

An effective TIP can help detect infiltrations more rapidly and provide your organization with a proactive approach to solving them. By importing threat data from multiple sources and formats, comparing that data, and then exporting it into an organization's existing ticketing systems or security systems, Threat Intelligence platform automates proactive threat management and mitigation.

Threat Intelligence Platform permits personnel throughout an enterprise to manage processes on the security relevant information that they care about. Processes might include conducting incident response, triaging events in the SOC or the threat team's processes for implementing external feeds or intelligence. From the management perspective, the platform must supply real-time updates, present trends and support threat-driven long-term prioritization across the business.

TIPs provide tools to help security analysts make an effective use of data accumulated on cyber threats globally. Threat Intelligence Platforms helps to solve the following challenges:

- Collecting a sufficient volume of useful data to understand the threat environment
- Automatically filtering out useless or non-actionable data, without human effort
- Contextualizing information to understand its importance
- Triaging actions to defend against threats and

alleviate risk in a timely manner

- Correlating data to view patterns and connections between active threats and possible vulnerabilities.

A mature TIP is used for operational day-to-day tackling and blocking, as well as process improvement and strategic decision making. Threat Intelligence platforms are made up of several key feature areas that allow organizations to integrate an intelligence-driven security approach. The core functions of a Threat Intelligence Platform are- aggregation, analysis and action.

Aggregation

Aggregation facilitates the collection, processing, analysis and exploitation stages of the Threat Intelligence Lifecycle. The platform gathers internal and external intelligence with the ability to parse and normalize cross-multiple sources including STIX, CSV, Custom XML/ JSON, IODEF, OpenIOC and many common formats, even e-mail.

Aggregation of Internal Intelligence

The Threat Intelligence Platform must ingest and store particular activities from SIEMs, select packet capture archives, incident response reports, malware and any internally derived intelligence reports. Typically, incoming feed information must be correlated with the organization's threat repository, and customized to meet the requirements of the different stakeholders – ranging from security team personnel to management and beyond.

Aggregation of External Intelligence

The Threat Intelligence Platform needs to ingest manifold sources of data, such as feeds of indicators (premium and open source, organized data with context, such as IODEF, STIX and emails, OpenIOC and intelligence reporting). The TIP should be able to interrogate other sources for indicator and file reputation, such as VirusTotal, blacklists, etc. It should be capable enough to gather information on indicator enhancement, for example IPGEO (geographical data).

A Threat Intelligence Platform allows analyst-driven and automated outward pivoting. Pivoting is a unique technique to place information in context by connecting it to other threat activities, and external pivoting monitors outer information such as malware repositories, DNS and domain intelligence.

Normalization and Parsing

The main challenge of aggregating Threat Intelligence is finding a method to approach the wide range of intelligence sources that are available. A Threat Intelligence Platform should be able to normalize and parse unstructured information, such as Office documents, blogs, PDFs, and text. It should also be competent to normalize and parse structured data such as IODEF, CSV, Custom XML/JSON, and OpenIOC.

Collecting Threat Intelligence

Cyber Threat Intelligence is a critical defense strategy in today's vigorous cyber threat landscape. As such, there has been an outburst of potential sources delivering a mind-boggling amount of information. The four subtypes of Cyber Threat Intelligence proposed are quite unique in terms of their collection, processing, analysis and consumption. Now let's address on how to collect the four subtypes of Threat Intelligence to the best effect.

Strategic Threat Intelligence Collection

Strategic cyber intelligence provides senior leaders with an accurate appraisal on how to direct cyber-related expenses in line with an organization's risk catechistic. Leveraging strategic intelligence to address strategic information requirements enables an organization to effectually assess, explicate, and quantify risk to senior management and stakeholders.

Strategic intelligence collection often requires assimilating information concerning political affairs, economics, societal interactions and technological developments. It usually evolves over a long timeframe and results in the development of intelligence estimates and studies.

As strategic Threat Intelligence is high-level, the larger part of the collection sources will be high-level as well. However, they are most likely to involve:

High-Level Geopolitical Appraisal

Trends in country tactics, priorities, ambitions and other superior-level information can help inform strategic analysis. Information to feed analysis will consequently come from high-level sources. This might include a scrutiny of policy releases by nations or groups of interest, news stories in foreign and domestic press, as well as news updates in subject-specific press, such as financial papers.

Most of the information required for analysis can be gathered from so called open source intelligence (OSINT). It has been noted that in the mixed-source report, open source intelligence often provides majority of the content. This can be a highly beneficial area of collection and should be dynamically pursued. For deep insight, organizations are entitled to ensure that they are not restricting searches to their own language or with a prejudice towards their own language. Using search engines like Google and Microsoft Bing can allow searching and collection of news articles, stories, policy, etc. directly from the foreign group of interest or nation. Moreover, the foreign language versions of Wikipedia may contain far more pertinent information than does the English language version.

Collection of strategic information is quite challenging as it requires a socio-political mind-set rather than a technical one. With such a massive amount of sources available, determining those that are both reliable and useful can be difficult. Therefore, many organizations prefer to acquire analysis directly from strategic intelligence providers. Generally, these providers endeavour general collection and analysis to produce products based on the client's requirements on a large proportion. However, since they are creating a relatively comprehensive product, the purchased analysis must be considered by an organization as congregated information, which is then scrutinized by the organization's own Cyber Threat Intelligence team.

Another major issue an analyst has to consider is the reliability of the information collected. A core source of information to help inform strategic analysis comes in the form of blog posts or white papers covering particular threat actors or attack campaigns. A cumulative number of white papers are being released and the information availed can help to build a clear picture of attack groups and their targets.

Human Contacts

Human contacts are tremendously useful while collecting strategic intelligence. Organizations in other sectors that have been in similar situations, or contacts at similar organizations, can provide valuable information on threats or attacks. The depth of information delivered by contacts will undoubtedly be proportional to the level of trust in that rapport, and so these interrelationships are worth developing and maintaining, even when no information is currently being sought.

Information should be treated sensitively. It is often better not to trait the information received to particular individuals. If it is essential to ascertain the source, then that information should itself be reliably protected.

Operational Threat Intelligence Collection

Operational Threat Intelligence is actionable information on specific inbound attacks or events. Operational intelligence appraises specific, potential incidents related to investigations, events, or activities, and provides insights that can support response operations. Idyllically, it informs on the nature of the attack, the competency and identity of the attacker –and gives a hint of when the attack is likely to take place.

Collecting operational intelligence in traditional realm will include activities such as compromise of the groups' communications and recruiting human sources within the groups. Operational Threat Intelligence for private enterprises is essentially restricted, as the majority of approaches of collecting such intelligence would be illegal for a private company. Organizations planning to conduct monitoring operations are directed to take legitimate advice before doing so. Inspecting open communications by groups is more likely to be legal than other approaches, yet organizations are recommended to seek advice in these cases too.

Activity-Related Attacks

In many cases, cyclical attacks could be correlated to real-world events, such as the activities of an organization related to finances or supports. This is a well-defined phenomenon in physical security, where – for instance – premises are attacked in response to certain triggers, and the same can be factual with regards to cyber-attacks. Analysts should aggregate information on threats or attacks, especially on those that are repetitive in nature such as DDoS attacks. Analysts should examine whether the information collected can be correlated to events or activities. Indicators on emerging attack should also be sought: for instance, social media posts.

Social Media

Another mode of garnering operational Threat Intelligence is to inspect social networks for indications of your organization in relation to a pre-planned attack. For instance, Twitter has a well-documented Application Program Interface (API) that can be utilized to set up a streaming feed, where all public tweets that match particular search terms are delivered through the API and can then be consumed and sieved by scripts. Conversely, the feeds of certain individuals who might tweet threats contrary to your organization can, once identified, be tracked.

Chat Rooms

Some intellectually motivated consortiums discuss plans in chat rooms. However, groups are often aware that these chats rooms are monitored and therefore confer more targeted operations in private chat rooms. It can be legally and operationally difficult to acquire access to these rooms. This is because many organizations will be restricted to the public rooms that are used to discuss larger-scale attacks - usually those that require a huge number of participants, such as DDoS (Denial of Service attack).

Organizations planning to actively collect information by participating in forums or chat rooms, must conduct such activities tactfully. However, this can be achieved by using non-attributable IP addresses and thwarting the leakage of other indicators.

Organizations should be cognizant that certain chat rooms used to confer wide-ranging attacks are in foreign terminology, thus surging the price of collection. There are many Threat Intelligence vendors who vend accumulated information from both private and public chat rooms. Prospective buyers need to ensure that the information being acquired is both legal and pertinent to their business.

Tactical Threat Intelligence Collection

Tactical Threat Intelligence is amongst the most beneficial forms of intelligence in terms of defending the organization. Tactical Threat Intelligence is information that deals with the tactics, techniques and procedures used by threat groups – including their tools and methodologies. Typically, tactical Threat Intelligence is employed by defenders such as administrators, architects and security staff.

Tactical Threat Intelligence collection is likely to emanate from mid-level sources, such as reports into attack campaigns. This level of intelligence requires focusing on the tactics of threats. And therefore, collection should target on sources that offer insight into these tactics.

Attack Campaign Reports

In the current threat environment, reports on specific actors or attack campaigns are the most frequently available sources, capable of providing information on tools and tactics. Moreover, efforts should be made to gather all information that are available. Staying abreast of documents posted on CiSP (Cyber-security Information Sharing Partnership) is an easy and effectual way to collect the majority of reports.

Malware

Evaluating malware samples from groups that have attacked the organization or similar organizations can avail valuable information on tools or tactics. Malware can be aggregated from feeds (either paid-for or free) that collect and disseminate malware. Conversely, a number of consortiums conduct malware analysis and release reports, which can be collected.

Incident Reports

Reports of incidents can help inform tactical analysis. In many cases, incident reports will be legally published as they appear in forums. However, informal incident reports can also be beneficial and worthy of collections. Incident Reports can take the form of conversations with investigators or defenders on the nature of attacks and the developments in approaches.

Technical Threat Intelligence Collection

Technical Threat Intelligence includes technical information of an attacker's assets, such as C2 channels, tools and infrastructure. This form of details usually is produced in the form of data and is normally consumed by technical means. Technical Threat Intelligence focuses on particular indicators, hasty distribution and response, and therefore has a shorter functional lifespan. An attacker using a particular piece of malware would be Tactical Threat Intelligence, while an indicator against a specific accumulated example would be Technical Threat Intelligence.

Perfect examples of Technical Threat Intelligence include document lures, subject headers of phishing emails, domain names used by C2 or IP addresses for C2endpoints. By swiftly including these indicators in defensive infrastructure such as endpoint security solutions, mail filtering devices and firewalls, enterprises can seek to detect attackers in the initial stages of an attack. Historical attacks can also be detected by searching logs of previously observed binaries or connections.

A major challenge faced by organizations endeavouring Technical Threat Intelligence is that the sheer amount of data can rapidly become devastating. In this occasion, the allocation of resources needs to be prudently considered, with the organization possibly becoming more selective in the data it gathers. There is also an apprehension that huge amounts of data vended as Technical Threat Intelligence lack contextual information, and therefore cannot feed higher analysis and assessment of sources.

Technical Threat Intelligence should be employed in an automated manner and placed into rulesets for endpoint security solutions or network security devices.

However, it's significant that capability development and resource allocation is incessantly balanced against an appraisal of the advantages of technical intelligence.

There are several types of data that can be categorized as Technical Threat Intelligence, with some indicators sturdy than others for adversaries to amend in their attempts to defeat signatures. This segment deals with the most commonly sought types. Indicators are usually collected from feeds, provided by third parties as a result of their investigations. Let's have a look at it in detail.

Malware Indicators

Malware indicators are often sought as Threat Intelligence since a major proportion of attacks involve malware. It is inconsequential for an attacker to alter their malware to avoid detection. Indicators such as file artifacts or created registry keys can be more beneficial, as they are less commonly modified by attackers. Nevertheless, it is still possible for an attacker to give dropped files a random or pseudorandom module in their name.

Campaign reports will contain indicators that can be treated as Technical Threat Intelligence. Lamentably, these indicators will often be included in PDF reports and therefore, collection encompasses copying and pasting the indicators before configuring them appropriately. There are many openly available and commercial feeds of malware indicators. Prior to collection, the content of feeds need be assessed meticulously to ensure they comprise litigable data.

Network Indicators

A number of diverse network indicators can be aggregated as Technical Threat Intelligence, as malware often needs to communicate with the attack consortium. Adversaries will operate nodes to conduct attacks and will occasionally use the same node for manifold victims. An IP address functioning as a C2 node can, therefore, be a beneficial indicator. However, adversaries will often use diverse IP addresses, fluctuating C2 nodes as they are detected or as computers become inaccessible.

As with malware indicators, network indicators can be discovered in reports and white papers. Yet again, a number of paid-for or freely available feeds exist.

Email Indicators

Email indicators can provide useful Threat Intelligence. A huge number of attacks begin with a phishing or spear phishing attack covering either a document exploit or merely malware camouflaged as something benevolent. Adversaries will often assure that emails are either targeted or semi-targeted. Therefore, generalist feeds of junk email subjects will be less valuable than details of phishing emails sent to parallel organizations.

It is advisable contacting analogous organizations in an effort to establish relationships in which the subject headers or other indicators of skeptical emails can be shared.

The ultimate goal of Threat Intelligence collection and sharing should be, as follows:

- Develop litigable intelligence
- Both internal and external sources need to address targeted threats or attacks.
- Better intelligence transforming to better protection
- Augmented protection transforming to less deception and decrease in revenue loss

Threat Intelligence Gathering Components

There are few major components of Threat Intelligence gathering that include:

Contractual Threats Specialist

There are many companies specialized in Cyber Threat Intelligence and organizations can contract with one of those specialized companies to avail some kind of regular available reports.

Data Analytics

A second major component of the Threat Intelligence gathering includes Data Analytics. Threat

Intelligence requires filtering through high volumes of data. And therefore, big data analytics is a beneficial tool to monitor for abnormal activities in the millions, or even trillions of data points flowing through organizational servers on a daily basis.

Community involvement

The final component of the Threat Intelligence gathering is community involvement. Over the past several years, the domain of cyber security has experienced a transmutation of sorts whereby Threat Intelligence or even security risk management approaches are not considered as trade secrets. Instead, security professionals perceive threat detection and vulnerability management as industry needs, community needs and even country level needs.

Selecting Data Sources

Gathering data helps you identify and detect the activity of potential adversaries in your environment. Typically, one can get effectual Threat Intelligence from a variety of diverse sources. Nevertheless, security monitoring feeds is broadly classified into five high-level categories:

1. Compromised Devices

This data source provides external notification

stating that a device is acting skeptically by participating in botnet-like activities or communicating with known bad sites. Services are actually evolving to excavate large volumes of Internet traffic to detect such devices.

2. Malware Indicators

Malware investigation continues to mature swiftly, getting better and better at understanding exactly what malicious code does to devices. This allows you to define both behavioural and technical indicators to monitor for within your environment.

3. IP Reputation

This is the most common reputation data source that provides a dynamic list of known bad or suspicious IP addresses. IP reputation has evolved since its initiation, and now features scores to correlate the analogous maliciousness of diverse addresses, as well as allocates additional context to further refine reputation.

4. Command and Control Networks

Intelligence on command and control (C2) networks is one of the specialized type of reputation often packaged as a separate feed. These feeds usually track global C2 traffic and identify botnet controllers, malware originators and other IP addresses and sites that you should look for while monitoring your environment.

5. Phishing Messages

Progressive attacks seem to start with a simple email.

The ubiquitousness of email and the ease of adding links to messages, enables adversaries to typically use email as the path of slightest resistance to a foothold in your environment. Segregating and analyzing phishing email can yield valuable information about the attacker's tools, tactics and procedures.

The above mentioned security data types are available in a variety of packages. Below are the main categories:

1. Commercial Integrated

Every security vendor is likely to have a research group offering some sort of intelligence. Generally, this data is tightly integrated into their product or service. Occasionally, there is a separate charge for the intelligence, and otherwise it is bundled into the product or service.

2. Commercial Standalone

An emerging security market for standalone Threat Intelligence has been currently witnessed. To this end, security vendors usually offer an aggregation platform for gathering external data and incorporating it into controls and monitoring systems. Some even collect industry-specific data as attacks likely to cluster around specific industries.

3. Information Sharing and Analysis Centers

Information Sharing and Analysis Centers (ISAC) are industry-specific organizations that collect data for an industry and share it amongst the members. The well-known Information Sharing and Analysis Center is for the financial sector, even though many other industry associations are spiralling up their own ISAC as well.

4. OSINT

Ultimately, open source intelligence (OSINT) includes a wide variety of publicly available sources for things like IP reputations and malware samples, which can be incorporated directly into other systems.

Categories of Threat Information

Threat information refers to any information pertinent to a threat that might enable an organization to protect itself against a threat or detect the activities of an actor. Major categories of threat information include the following:

1. Threat Indicators

Threat indicators, or indicators of compromise (IOC), are technical artifacts or observables that indicate the possibility of an attack or compromise of some kind. Indicators can be used to identify and defend against potential or existing threats. Perfect examples of indicators include the IP address of a suspected C2 server, a URL that references malicious content, a file hash for a malicious executable, a suspicious DNS domain name or the subject line text of a malicious email message. Among these, the most common types are file hashes and reputation data on domains and IP addresses that have been allied with attacks.

2. File Hashes and Reputation Data

A malware file hash is an identifier of a particular virus; Trojan, rootkit, worm, keylogger, or other kind of malicious code. The file known to contain malware creates a unique "fingerprint" based on the series of bytes in the file. IP addresses, URL reputations and Domains are risk ratings of computers and webpages on the Internet. Typically, high risk scores are allocated to websites and systems associated with:

- Spam
- Spyware and Malware
- Phishing and other frauds
- peer-to-peer (P2P) networking and anonymous proxy tools
- Command and control (C2) servers
- Data exfiltration servers
- Botnets
- Internet Protocol addresses that cannot be traced

Reputation scores can also be assigned to websites and computers that have been compromised, even if they are not fully under the control of a malevolent actor.

3. Threat Data Feeds

Threat data feeds provide highly contextual information to build proactive defense strategies, triage alerts and resources as well as enhance incident response. The primary value of threat data feeds is to enhance the efficacy of next-generation firewalls(NGFW), secure web gateways(SWGs), intrusion prevention system(IPSs), anti-spam and anti-malware packages and other blocking technologies.

Threat data feeds include statistical break down on the prevalence, targets and sources of common attack and malware activities. Threat data feeds help security teams discover patterns linked with attacks.

Cyber Threat Statistics, Reports and Surveys

The cyber security industry is chock-full of statistics, surveys and reports that constantly provide new insights and stats. Statistics, reports and surveys help security teams to emphasize on the most rampant attacks and alert them to emerging threats.

Statistics

Being the science of information collection, scrutiny and interpretation, statistics is a vital tool for cyber threat analysis. Cyber security vendors provide statistics on spam, botnets, malware and other elements of cyber-attacks. Numerous statistical methods are being employed within the Threat Intelligence reports issued by the vendors.

Reports and Surveys

Threat Intelligence reports are prose documents

that generally describe threat actors, TTPs, types of systems being targeted, and other threat-related data that offers better situational awareness to an organization. A number of consulting firms and vendors publish detailed reports and surveys on various aspects of cyber security and cyber threats. The reports usually include:

- Trends and Statistics on diverse types of attacks
- Analysis from experts
- Survey results

Survey data is very beneficial as it gives a clear picture of the experiences, successes, and failures of IT companies in responding to threats effectively.

Malware Analysis

Malware analysis is a method by which cyber-security experts inspect malicious software present in a computer system. Malware analysis offers valuable insights into the demeanour of malware samples and the intent of the attackers. The malware is broken up into key components in order to scrutinize its behavior. Usually this can be done in two ways:

Dynamic Malware Analysis:

Dynamic malware analysis is performed by monitoring the behavior of the malware while it is actually running on a host system. Technical indicators divulged with basic dynamic analysis can include IP addresses, file path locations, domain names, registry keys, and additional files found on the system or network. This form of analysis is often performed in a sandbox environment to thwart the malware from infecting production systems.

The most accurate malware analysis is delivered by sandboxing technology or dynamic analysis. With sandboxing, a skeptical file is permitted to run in a virtual execution environment sequestered from the corporate network. The sandboxing product monitors and documents all of the actions performed by the file, including malevolent activities such as:

- Deactivating antivirus software on the system
- Making anomalous entries to the registry
- Searching on the network for archives whose names include "admin" or "password"
- Making callouts to C2 servers on the web
- Linking to servers used to stage and exfiltrate filched data

The observed behaviors not only demonstrate whether the sample is malicious or not, but also provide indication about the attacker's goals and tactics.

Static Malware Analysis

Static malware analysis is performed by dichotomizing the different resources of the binary archive without executing it and reviewing each component. In short, static analysis scrutinizes malware without viewing the actual instructions or code. This form of analysis employs different techniques and tools to rapidly determine whether a file is malicious or not, and provide valuable information about its functionality and gather technical indicators to create simple signatures. Technical indicators collected with basic static analysis can include file name, file type, file size, hashes and recognition by antivirus detection tools.

Thus, threat data feeds can improve your security posture by providing the following services:

Malware Defense

The dissemination of malicious objects can be clogged at the infrastructure level by adding the MD5 message-digest hashes to the blackballs of network level accesses and firewalls.

Web-based Infection Prevention

By adding the URLs and corresponding masks into blackballs of network level gateways and firewalls, Malicious URLs can be blocked.

Up-to-date

Intelligence Feed databases are updated frequently with the state-of-the-art results correlated from the cloud network and other sources.

Cyber Threat Intelligence - Threat Intelligence Analysis

Intelligence: Collecting, Analyzing Threat, Evaluating

Threat Intelligence is one of the business priorities that gained importance from the past 6 years. Understanding and applying crucial intelligence for cyber threats is defined as 'Threat Intelligence'. General awareness of Threat Intelligence has grown dramatically in search engines. Understanding 'Threat Intelligence' starts from collecting information that can be acted upon to change outcomes. In addition, analyzing and evaluating different possibilities defines the act of Threat Intelligence. Threat Intelligence is a broad topic with numerous sub-categories that narrows down to different threats and builds more informed definition of solutions for the threats.

The various types of Threat Intelligence include:

Strategic Threat Intelligence –The highest level of information consumed by senior decision-makers or prime decision makers. It may or may not be technical but will for sure comprise of financial impact of cyber activity. They are part of conversations in form of documentation and records.

Operational Threat Intelligence – It is the information collected on prediction of a specific attack against the organization that necessitates higher-level security staff. Operational Threat Intelligence narrows down to the understanding of the group that is involved in attack against the organization. They state when, how and sort of intelligence required to immune the organization from the Threat. The kind of Threat is rare and normally confined to the government level.

Tactical Threat Intelligence – Tactics, Techniques and Procedures (TTP's) and information on how the threat is going to be executed on the organization can be referred to as Tactical Threat Intelligence. Incident reports generate information on such Threats.

Technical Threat Intelligence –The information in the form of data consumed through technical means can be defined as Technical Threat Intelligence. The suspected IP address, website or the server that is malicious are part of Technical information. The timeline of the Threat Intelligence is normally short since the attackers can effortlessly change the IP addresses.

The main proposed subtypes of Threat Intelligence course of action are collection, analysis and evaluation. These actions will address the issues and provide guidance understanding and executing the intelligence for the best effect.

The proper analysis of Threat Intelligence will benefit the organization at all levels by improving the security of their business.

Collecting Cyber Threat Information

Collection is the primary and vital step that dominates Cyber Threat Information. Collecting the information is the only lead to the next step of analyses. The information can be derived from a wide variety of sources, such as news feeds, forums, paid-for services or feeds, or even human sources. As mentioned, the collection and analysis of Threat Intelligence information is challenging and requires a socio-political mindset along with technical understanding. With numerous resources available for identifying the solutions for the problematic threats, establishing a viewpoint to represent the trend or intention will depend on the collection of information.

Information alone cannot be the intelligence, but it is the raw material that leads to the path of intelligence through the produced analysis. An organization has a huge cyber database of threat information like the logs, malware signatures, and other indicators of compromise. Analysis of strategic intelligence providers can streamline the information.

Cyber threat information can be cracked with the help of threat indicator, or indicator of negotiation. The threat indicator is an entity that indicates the possibility of an attack or negotiation for a solution. The Malware file hash is one of the unique identifier of the virus, worm, Trojan, rootkit, key loggers, and other types of malicious codes. Most prevalent types of attacks are file hashes i.e., signatures, reputation of data on domains and IP addresses.

The process location can be done by creating networks of honeypots, tracking web server activities with the help of a computer, email servers, and other systems and tracking the users surfing the web. The sensors will collect files and emails that interrupt the corporate systems and the users during the course of normal operations.

The Risk rates are high for computers and web pages when it comes to domain, IP address, and URL reputations. Reputation scores can be assigned to computers and websites even if they are not under any threat. In most situations, the malicious activities are proof of threats used by hackers on a domain of a website or a system

Threat data feeds derived from the server and computer system provides information that correlates and analyzes threat indicators. Thus, the concerned organization's security team can identify the patterns associated with attacks.

The compressive statistics, reports, and surveys will guide the security team to focus on the most common attacks, and further alert them on emerging threats. The insight Malware analysis gives the behavioral pattern of malware samples and the vital intentions of the attackers. The detailed automated malware analysis of dynamic analysis or sandboxing technology helps to observe and document all the actions in a virtual environment and corporate network.

With sandboxing, suspicious malicious activities can be detected from unusual entries in the registry, disabled antivirus software on the system and locating the network affected by files. The observed behaviors are not samples but evidence about the attacker's goals. Sandboxing alone cannot identify unknown malware, since advanced malware files evade sandboxing technologies.

All the media for exchanges including online forums, email, instant messaging platforms, social media, and full featured online stores, digital assets, including credit card and Social Security numbers, personal information, and login credentials are subjected to malware activities. Most of the online activities are public, thus they become subject to phishing campaigns attacks, and other malicious tools and techniques.

Attacks and campaigns are executed through cyberattack tools with fake website design, and password cracking. While visiting these websites, it is always suggested to brush up on your language skills. Once the researchers crack the motivation and intention of the attack, they will be able to collect a wide variety of information. Thus, motivation and intentions serve as evidence of adversaries that are likely to attack the industry or enterprise. Further, the motivations and intentions will help in assessing the target. The motivation of the cybercriminals is to make a profit but some of the intentions can vary with the attacks.

There are numerous varieties of exhibited range of motivations and intentions that include stealing the product designs, intellectual property, and business plans, breaking open the bid details and proposals, and obtaining, political and defense-related intelligence.

Typically, several ways can be adopted to gather threat data. For an easy-to-understand approach, data collection can be broadly classified into three main categories - passive, hybrid and active collections.

Passive Collection

Data gathered on networks or information systems for which you possess accountability fall under passive collection. The term passive here represents an analyst who is not engaging directly with an adversary or their infrastructure. The perfect examples would be analysts tracking internal company forums, capturing internal network traffic, accumulating system logs and other interior activities of an enterprise such as execution of red team assessments.

Hybrid Collection

Hybrid data collection is a pivotal aspect of Cyber Threat Intelligence. Typically, it moves into the realm of data dissemination, liaison and threat-intelligence reporting amid allied governments or industry peers who may be vulnerable to a shared or parallel adversarial threat. The best example of Hybrid data collection would be the establishment of a honeypot, a technique used to collect further information on adversary intention and motives.

Active Collection

Active data collection involves gleaning data from information systems or external networks that are under the dominance of an adversary. An outstanding example of active data collection would be a command and control server being employed to correlate to malware. This category of data collection must be implemented astutely so that the legal and privacy rights of affiliates are secure.

After deciding on the category of data collection to be performed, it is vital to comprehend the type of data collected. Normally, data can be categorized into three forms- Raw data, Exploited data and Production data.

Raw Data

Raw Data are unevaluated data gathered from a repository. This kind of data can be the most prolific one but demands ample time to process and appraise it. For example, it includes raw details such as network logs, IP addresses, network architecture maps, or full forum posts by a possible adversary. Usually, this sort of data can be found in the second phase of the Threat Intelligence lifecycle.

Exploited Data

Exploited Data are those data processed and scrutinized by another expert and it encompasses designated raw data. Ideal examples would be IPS Alerts/

anti-virus on networks, malware reports with samples, technical reports from other networks, or campaign reports. This is the sort of data that will be accessible to an analyst after the third stage of the Threat Intelligence lifecycle.

Production Data

Production Data refers to those data that are finalized into a report destined for distribution. This may either include limited or no raw data. Furthermore, production data may be destined for the awareness of a reader or customer or it might be proposed for planned actions. Best examples would include data such as campaign reports without samples, government tips, advisories and malware reports without samples. This kind of data will be accessible only after the fourth stage of the intelligence life cycle.

Intelligence Collection Disciplines

The collection of information is a crucial element of the intelligence process. There are five main ways of gathering intelligence that are often referred to as intelligence collection disciplines. Every intelligence discipline is utilized to collect information regarding specific threats or attacks. The most common types of these techniques include open source intelligence (OSINT), human intelligence (HUMINT), signals intelligence (SIGINT), imagery intelligence (IMINT), and measurement and signatures intelligence (MASINT).

Open Source Intelligence (OSINT)

Open Source Intelligence is the process of gathering a broad array of information and sources from publicly available resources such as television, newspapers, radio, journals, the Internet, commercial databases, and graphics, videos, and drawings. Typically, open source materials can provide information on organizational dynamics, technical procedures and research activities available in any form. One of the main advantages of OSINT is its availability, while the sheer quantity of accessible information can make it hard to know what is of value.

Human Intelligence (HUMINT)

Human intelligence is a category of intelligence derived from individuals or humans by evaluating behavioural responses via direct interaction. This information, however, includes all kinds of intelligence amassed by humans ranging from direct inspection and monitoring to the use of recruited agents. Human intelligence can accumulate information that is intricate or sometimes implausible to collect by other technical means. Collection of information via human source includes covert, overt and clandestine approach.

Signals Intelligence (SIGINT)

Signals Intelligence is a generic term used to collect intelligence by intercepting communication signals and electronic signals transmitted by personal computers, cell phones, and telephones. SIGINT includes both the raw data and the scrutiny of the data. Signals intelligence can be categorized into three sub-disciplines: Electronic Intelligence, Communications Intelligence and Foreign Instrumentation Signals Intelligence.

Imagery Intelligence (IMINT)

Imagery Intelligence is kind of intelligence derived from visual photography, infrared sensors, radar, electro-optics, thermal and multi-spectral sensors. Generally, it includes depictions of objects reproduced either electronically or by optical means or other media. Both the types of imagery sources i.e., soft- and hard-copy imagery can be appraised and construed for numerous purposes by varied users. Furthermore, IMINT includes the exploitation of information to discover, categorize, and identify objects or organizations.

Measurement and Signatures Intelligence (MASINT)

Measurement and Signature Intelligence is a technically derived intelligence acquired by the quantitative and qualitative analysis of technical data related with any source, sender or emitter. The data is evaluated and results in intelligence that locates, recognizes, or delineates distinctive features of specific targets. Examples of MASINT disciplines include nuclear intelligence (NUCINT), infrared intelligence (IRINT), and radar intelligence (RADINT).

Components of Threat Intelligence Collection

Below are few major components of Threat Intelligence collection:

Contractual Threats Specialist

There are several organizations that are specialized in Cyber Threat Intelligence. Therefore, enterprises can enter into contract with one of those specialized organizations to acquire some kind of systematic available reports.

Data Analytics

Data Analytics is the second pivotal component of the Threat Intelligence collection. Threat Intelligence entails sieving through high volumes of data. Consequently, big data analytics is an advantageous tool to observe for anomalous activities through the millions of data points flowing through organizational servers on a regular basis.

Community Involvement

Community Involvement is the ultimate component of the Cyber Threat Intelligence collection. The realm of cyber security has experienced a transmutation of sorts in the last several years. As a result, Threat Intelligence or even security risk management methodologies are not considered as trade secrets. Also, security experts consider threat discovery and vulnerability management as community needs, industry needs and even country level needs.

Therefore, Threat Intelligence in the corporate world is constrained by the technologies, nature of the information collected, sources of the information, authenticity of the data and the environmental coverage.

Cyber Threat Intelligence Analysis

In the current era of security threat attacks and cyber warfare, it comes as a vital need to persistently monitor and scrutinize the ongoing threats and day-to-day malicious activities. An essential component of Threat Intelligence analysis at any level is the competency to defeat prejudices and analysis of information. Converting data into information thatbecome useful requires an analysis to be conducted. In certain cases, analysis will be simple, for instance, scrutinizing a feed into a firewall deny-and-alert ruleset. While in other cases, it involves extracting the pertinent information from a bigger work, such as a report, and comprehending which components apply to the organization's assets.

As a generic knowledge-based activity, analysis can be disintegrated into taxonomy of sub-types that encompasses categorization, parsing, evaluation, monitoring and prediction. During the analysis stage, raw data is converted into information in the form of trends, patterns, clusters, sequences and so on. However, this task is accomplished via a sequence of primitive implications such as selection, cataloguing, abstraction, specification, decomposition, matching, comparison, instantiation, inter connection and transformation. If the information produced during the analysis phase provides necessary understanding for extenuating a perilous event then it can be termed as intelligence.

Cyber Threat Intelligence is the output of analysis based on identification, accumulation, and enhancement of pertinent data and information. Usually, the analysis consists of findings, facts and forecasts that delineate the element of study and allow the appraisal and anticipation of events and consequences. The analysis should be unbiased, opportune, and most significantly accurate. A key role for the analyst is to seek for opportunities to produce new kinds of intelligence through a blend from current intelligence. For instance, an analyst might spend quality time reading through white papers to extract IOCs that can be bestowed to network defenders. After reading such papers, the analyst might discover trends that can be drawn together into a tactical intelligence product for upper management.

More often, an interplay between collection and analysis process occurs when analysts understand that the collection is not providing the required raw material; or possibly that different information needs to be accumulated for appropriate analysis. Typically, the analysts implement four basic types of reasoning to produce intelligence accurately. These include deduction, induction, abduction and the scientific method. The analyst should be conscious of the diverse analytical pitfalls, as bias and misperceptions can influence the analysis to a larger extent. And therefore, the result is a value-added litigable information customized to a specific need.

Analytical Strategies

Analysis is performed by implementing a blend of human analysts and machines. Machines usually perform simpler, high volume chores that reduce a huge quantity of input data down to a more manageable subdivision. Later on, human analysts apply a crucial level of judgement to this sieved data to ensure that the ultimate intelligence product contains minimum false positives.

Depending on the intelligence requirements, analytical strategies can either be hypothesis-driven or data-driven. During the data-driven analysis, machines play a leading number-crunching role. While during hypothesis-driven analysis, human analysts apply their curiosity, intuition and imagination. Hypothesis-driven analysis is the most effective and powerful approach as it is backed by a combination of innovative human and systematic machine.

Machine-based Analytical Methods

Employing machines to carry out or support Threat

Intelligence analysis is considered a mature discipline. Based on the type of threat being analyzed, machine-based analytical techniques are categorized as follows:

Known Knowns

Generally, these are threats formerly encountered and identified by means of discovering similar attributes. Based on an analyst's knowledge and tech-savvy, it can be expressed in the form of a production rule or other form of machine-executable procedure.

Unknown Knowns

Unknown knowns are threats that are known about but have never been witnessed, or have been previously witnessed but are not found at present because of altered attributes. However, they can be discovered using matching techniques such as:

- Hard matching - It is a technique where a threat is discovered by matching against a repeated identifier.

- Fuzzy matching - Under this technique, repeat identifiers are resolved through a fuzzier form of matching. Nevertheless, this returns a list of results depending on likely relevance though the exact spellings or words may not match exactly.

- Geo-matching - It is a technique where

geolocation data is used for identifying clusters of significant activity or hotspots.

- Social network analysis – Under this technique, networks of new, unknown threats are identified based on its association with other, known, threats.

Unknown Unknowns

Unknown unknowns are threats that have not been formerly encountered. However, they can be identified by implementing two types of techniques:

- Supervised learning - It is a technique where threat attributes are induced by the machine (in the form of rules) based on historical examples where the result (threat or no threat) is known.

- Unsupervised learning - Under this method, the machine applies an automated learning technique on a huge quantity of data in order to identify threat attributes for itself.

Components of Cyber Threat Analysis as a Process

Threat analysis is a practice under which the knowledge of external and internal information vulnerabilities related to a specific organization are matched against real-world cyber-attacks. This threat-oriented approach to combat cyber-attacks exemplifies a smooth evolution from a state of reactive security to a state of proactive one. Besides, the preferred outcome of a threat analysis is to give best practices on how to maximize the defensive instruments pertaining to availability, reliability, and confidentiality. Now let's have a brief look at the components of cyber threat analysis.

Scope

Scope provides information regarding what is included and what is not included in the analysis process. With respect to cyber security, items under consideration are those that must be protected adeptly. Though they need to be discovered on priority, the level of sensitivity of what is being protected should be well-defined by analysis drafters.

Data Collection

Almost all leading organizations adopt some kind of policies and procedures. However, these aspects need to be identified for acquiescence purposes.

Gathering comprehensive information regarding real cyber incidents is the first step. But the key focus should be on targeted threats existing in reality. The scope settings need to sift out those perceived but not real, as it can just divert the attention from other ongoing security activities.

An analyst must have free access to data in order to convert it into intelligence. Sources of information, however, comprises detection of system logs, firewall logs, intrusion incidents, open source internet searches, honeypots, digital forensic analysis, the reverse engineering of malware, etc. Certainly, one source cannot provide all of the information required for a detailed threat investigation, and therefore the analyst should integrate multiple data flawlessly. Once when all corporate policies and procedures are accumulated, they should be analyzed to illustrate whether they match the compliance level in the organization. Subsequently, processing huge amount of data and thinking analytically are attributes that will form a good cyber threat analysis.

Threat Analysis of Acceptable Risks

In this phase, the collected information is examined to determine the level of current exposure i.e., whether the current defenses are rigid enough to counteract information threats in terms of availability, reliability and confidentiality. This element also includes an appraisal of whether the existing security measures, procedures and policies are adequate.

Threat analysis is a continuous process that should be reviewed once in a while to ensure that all safety measures works properly. Moreover, threat analysis includes penetration testing, which in turn seeks to procure something valuable from the attacker's arsenal like a classified document, password or code.

Mitigation and Anticipation

When all the above mentioned steps are accomplished, a proficient security analyst can use this huge corpus of threat data to arrange in-group activity patterns of similarity, trait each pattern to particular threat actors, swiftly implement extenuation measures, and antedate the emergence of similar cyber-attacks in the future.

Analyzing Cyber Threat Intelligence

In today's vigorous cyber threat landscape, Threat Intelligence is a vital defense strategy. Intrinsically, there has been an outburst of prospective sources producing a mind-boggling amount of information. The four types of Threat Intelligence intended are quite unique in terms of their collection, analysis and consumption. Now let's address how to analyze the four subtypes of Threat Intelligence to the best effect.

Strategic Threat Intelligence Analysis

Strategic analysis can be a highly challenging one, as it's rare to deal with absolutes and more common to work with observations, trends and perceived intents. When compared to other areas of intelligence, Strategic Threat Intelligence analysis requires more expertise and probably a wider array of collected information. Collection and analysis are likely to be strongly correlated, with lines of investigation and trends identified and then authenticated by collecting new information.

Top companies will often recruit people with expertise in socio-political analysis or traditional intelligence and then train them on the cyber components crucial to perform effectual subject-specific analysis. On the other hand, technical staff in the intelligence team can be trained on Strategic analysis. However, this methodology requires a great deal of interpretation and understanding of the political and sociological background.

Meta-analysis is often considered as a beneficial component of strategic Threat Intelligence whereby results from a range of analyses are merged and reassessed in an effort to acquire new intelligence. This can be predominantly expedient with, for instance, technical white papers that come through the team. Attribution in cyber-attacks is often challenging. Henceforth, while they can sometimes prove beneficial, any specified attributions in a report should be treated with some caution. The stated range of industries to be targeted should also be monitored prudently, unless the methodologies for identifying victims are open to scrutiny.

Operational Threat Intelligence Analysis

Collected data of attacks are worth analyzing for indication of activity or event-related attacks. Analysts should endeavor to ascertain whether they are part of a pattern pertinent to events or activities, or to reported activities. It is vital to be cognizant that attacks could be linked not only to activities by the organization itself, but to those of partner organizations or individuals/groups that are in some or the other way interconnected to the organization.

Operational Threat Intelligence is not event-based, but it seems to focus on chat room conversations and social network posts. Typically, these repositories will be of high volume, with a great deal of 'noise'. And therefore organizations are advised to build scripts that discover messages of interest. Also, it can be advantageous for analysts to quest through the gathered data manually to find indications of attacks, and then build scripts that ensure analogous messages would be extracted in the future.

Groups can sometimes use codes or just slang that obfuscates meaning. In certain circumstances, these entail simple substitution, where a slang name is implemented for a certain target or type of attack. Analysts will have to make sure that they stay abreast of codes and slang, and that analytical script and wordlists are similarly updated. Another key aspect that an analyst needs to take into consideration is that individuals tend to change aliases on a daily basis. This might require more advanced monitoring, such as timeline analysis or linguistic analysis.

By merging operational Threat Intelligence with other forms of intelligence, deeper analysis can be achieved.

For instance, to ensure that there is a clear understanding of groups' competencies and methodologies, tactical intelligence can be merged into the operational Threat Intelligence output to produce more information on the projected form and scale of the attack.

Tactical Threat Intelligence Analysis

To extract indications of tactics, all gathered sources should be analyzed. Also, Reports and White papers can be deconstructed to determine the usage of particular tools and tactics. Predominantly, analysts should endeavor to identify:

Mode of Operation and Exploited Issues

Analysts should continue to make their best efforts to comprehend how threat actors are functioning while attacking networks. For instance, how did the attackers escalate privileges, how did they initially gain access, how did they move laterally in the network, and how did they extract data? For each stage in the process, individual attackers and even attack groups will have patterns of behaviour. Generally, these patterns exploit common issues on corporate networks, such as privileged accounts used to log into workstations or flat networks with no separation. Analysts should discover the issues exploited by adversaries and identify whether those issues are present on their own networks.

Tools

Intelligence on the tools utilized by adversaries can

inform both detection and protection. Attackers usually modify open source tools to elude trivial detection. Understanding the competencies of the tools in use is also imperative. Many adversaries use openly available Remote Access Tools (RATs), which is intelligence in itself, while some develop their own. Custom RATs should be scrutinized to determine the information that attackers are trying to acquire, and their competencies in this respect, to support detection.

Parsing of tools and diverse versions of those tools can give a hint of how advanced a specific actor is. Any change in an individual attacker tools or attack group's tools could denote a variation in its intentions and resourcing. Furthermore, analysts should aim to comprehend what the tool can do, and, potentially, what the tool says about the expertise of its creators and users.

Communications Techniques

Analysts should make an effort to understand the data exfiltration and C2 (Command & Control) channels used by attackers, and map that data onto their organization to comprehend whether it would be discovered or prevented. Attackers use HTTP or simple communications techniques in many circumstances, while in some cases they use complicated DNS as a command and control channel.

Forensic Avoidance Strategies

Analysts should be looking for insight into how

adversaries are attempting to avoid detection in their actions and tools. Many attackers do not make specific efforts in this regard, while some take substantial trouble to delay or avoid detection. Analysts are advised to find out the tactics implemented and establish how defenses can be adapted to overcome these stratagems.

Technical Threat Intelligence Analysis

More often, the analysis of technical Threat Intelligence will be automated or heavily automated. This is because indicators will have a short operational time before adversaries' makes changes, and therefore hasty filtering is vital.

Conversion between Formats

Technical Threat Intelligence can be transferred in a number of contending formats and tools that exist to convert one format into another for easy consumption. Generally, IOC formats are XML-based and are readily analyzed by scripts into a format appropriate for toolsets. However, Technical Threat Intelligence offered in formats that are native to particular tools will not require conversion.

In certain cases, indicators might just be a list of IP addresses or hashes that require formatting. Therefore, it is suggested that at least one analyst of the intelligence team should be able to script or program adeptly.

Technical Threat Intelligence Libraries

A 'Threat Intelligence library' is used to store indicators and seek links between them. Also, this approach enables an organization to discover attacks within logs and packet captures. These libraries often use so-called 'big data' technologies such as graph analysis and data warehousing in an attempt to draw links between the categories of Technical Threat Intelligence. This, however, allows swift response to identified threats, as well as a historical record of received Indicators of Compromises.

Threat Analyst and its Appraisal Abilities

The analyst approaches to ascertain the level of risk within his organization based on both vulnerability and risk appraisement. Furthermore, they have to define what security measures need to be taken and remove the ineffective ones. The analyst should be vigilant not to push onward with an overprotective security system, as it might prove unfoundedly expensive to the organization.

It is estimated that about 86% of security budgets available to cyber security teams are exhausted at the infiltration stage on warding off malevolent attempts. Most organizations face the issue of reducing false positives, an immanent occurrence in the evaluation of applications. The perfect way to mitigate the issue is to assure that applications in question are up-to-date with latest signatures and patches. Moreover, the data in hand is often derived from intelligence products.

Evidently the ability to parse security events is

the most significant set of skills that an analyst should possess. At times, this skill is not an exact science, but it is more like an art where the individual simply has to have a flair for it.

Making an accurate analysis goes hand in hand with the analyst's tech-savviness. For example, a security analyst who does not know routing protocols and infrastructure cannot analyze what happens when an adversary sends distorted TCP (Transmission Control Protocol) packets to an enterprises server. The same condition applies for a situation where the analyst cannot state the difference between an ineffectual zero-day and a zero-day that can perpetrate real damage.

On the other hand, analysts may sometimes produce a bad investigation that can be deceptive. Therefore, the analyst's competency to differentiate good from bad is vital here.

Cyber Threat Intelligence Evaluation

Evaluation is the most integrated part of the commercial "Threat Intelligence" ecosystem. The Threat Intelligence team should always ensure that the evaluation of the intelligence product meet its original requirements. If the requirements have been met, then the product can further feed the requirements to help develop new-fangled, deeper requirements that build upon the intelligence product – and then the Threat Intelligence lifecycle can repeat. If the acquired Threat Intelligence does not meet its requirements, then it denotes a failure at some point, and the cycle model can be utilized to establish where the failure has exactly occurred.

The threat evaluation is considered to be a vital part of the organization's overall life cycle. Repositories of intelligence information must be investigated for their usefulness, validity and fidelity. Validating sources and categorizing them as per their reliability will allow an analyst to make sound decisions and assessments of the data gathered.

Evaluation of Strategic Threat Intelligence

Strategic Threat Intelligence should be evaluated in an accurate, impactful and timely manner in order to support senior decision-makers. Accuracy can be difficult to appraise in absolute terms, but it's generally possible to appraise a product in terms of the intelligence team's specified belief in its accuracy. As for the intelligence product's impact, the question is how directly the product matches the stated requirements and how beneficial the product is in supporting decisions. Timeliness is nothing but ensuring whether the information is delivered to the consumer rapidly enough – and in a useable form.

Evaluation of Operational Threat Intelligence

When compared to other forms of intelligence, Operational Threat Intelligence is easy to evaluate. Intelligence is said to be successful if it was able to predict an attack in time and, as a result, the attack is wholly or partly mitigated. If the internal attacks were not predicted, it can therefore be advantageous to conduct some root cause analysis.

In most of the cases, the conclusion will be that accumulating the required information to provide forewarning would have been impossible or illegal. Whereas it would have been possible, if an inspection of the collection and analysis process will help to discover opportunities for future enhancement. Consequently, the on-going operational Threat Intelligence efforts should be evaluated strictly. There are few cases where good, actionable information is acquired – while resources might be better focused on other forms of Threat Intelligence.

Evaluation of Tactical Threat Intelligence

The evaluation of tactical Threat Intelligence should involve an appraisement of how well it feeds into the defensive procedures, and whether the hardening suggested by the intelligence team has mitigated or allowed the detection of specific attacks.

The methodologies of the attackers should be assessed when successful attacks have occurred. And a conclusion has to be drawn with regard to whether the organization should have been conscious of, and alleviated, the attack. For instance, if the attacker has implemented a rare technique, then it's implausible that collection would have been able to produce intelligence.

Evaluation of Technical Threat Intelligence

Technical Threat Intelligence can be a complicated endeavour – as it is quite expensive, if in case, feeds and diagnostic solutions are procured commercially. And therefore, they should be meticulously evaluated, specifically, the number of prevented attacks that would not have been obviated by any other means.

Many organizations seem to focus substantial proportions of their Threat Intelligence exertion on this particular area. This can prove ineffective, as by the nature of technical Threat Intelligence gathering, adversaries will always be capable of eluding detection by causing a more custom targeted attack. Therefore, evaluation should contemplate if resources would be better applied to other forms of Threat Intelligence.

Cyber Threat IntelligenceThreat Intelligence is a pivotal component of an adaptive security model. With so many distinct offerings and so much pressure, organizations take high risk investing huge amounts of time and money with little positive effect on intelligence-led security.

Despite their hefty budgets and time consuming implementation procedure, Cyber Threat Intelligence is adapted by many organizations. It supports an organization with the latest information that is required to comprehend and react to current threats while also working to thwart such attacks from occurring in the future.

Threat Intelligence is a popular term in the cyber security industry, and has become a catch-all phrase for an array of technologies and approaches. In an environment with tight budgets, the application of a CTI program implementing a phased and requirements-based approach can allow small investments to substantially boost the overall security posture of an organization.

Module 11
SOC - Cyber Threat Intelligence Program and Partners

Cyber Threat Intelligence Program

The upsurging speed and volume of vibrant and emerging threats has left organizations scrambling to efficiently respond. Cyber Threat Intelligence (CTI) is a dynamic process that allows an organization to persistently collect valuable insights based on the investigation of situational and contextual risks and can be customized to the organization's precise threat landscape. By integrating CTI into their security manoeuvres, top organizations can truncate the time involved in detection of pertinent threats and respond more efficiently.

In this corporate world, developing an effectual Cyber Threat Intelligence program is a pivotal step towards ensuring a sturdy information security strategy. A strong Threat Intelligence program bestows information about the entire operational environment and possible threats in a customized and easily understood format and thereby improves situational awareness. This will enable decision-makers to instantly comprehend the irresistible risks they face and how those risks could affect the organizations.

A CTI program is scalable in accordance with the size of a business. A powerful Threat Intelligence program needs to take into consideration all threats including geopolitical risk, industrial crime, civil unrest, terrorism, war, environmental trends and threats, social activism, cyber threats and corruption -all within the framework of its business strategy and operations. It should also look for internal threats such as abnormal patterns in incident reporting, poor or non-existent resiliency policies, the supply chain infrastructure, and the operations of business partners.

A vigorous CTI program can shed light on a myriad of crucial business concerns and risks, while proffering countermeasures, highly technical actions and metrics to the cyber security program at large. By empowering organizations to understand their external and internal threat environment, a CTI program can assist companies to accurately prepare for or avert a crisis before it occurs. Such an efficient program can alert decision-makers to forthcoming political or civil disruptions in unstable countries that could endanger the safety of employees and operations.

Despite its time consuming implementation process and tight budgets, CTI program is making its way into more organizations. There is no bullet-proof security approach and risk management, but through constant intelligence gathering and defense optimization, businesses can upsurge their protection. By developing a CTI program, leading organizations are able to instantaneously enhance existing cybersecurity practices and develop overarching insights into their particular threat landscape.

Steps in planning a CTI Program

- Decide on what's the purpose of the TI data, and who will be responsible for planning the CTI.

- After deciding upon the purpose of the TI data, the company will then need to choose the appropriate tools for data collection and accumulation. Additionally, the company need to decide on which data sources shall be used (external, internal, or both).

- The ultimate step in planning a Cyber Threat IntelligenceThreat Intelligence program is setting the goals, as well as the procedures for progress measurement. However, this can be grouped into long term and short term.

Components of a Successful CTI Program

An effective and successful CTI program entails both a strategic and an operational component. However, the strategic component includes the following:

Relationship Building

Exchanging threat information with authentic communities such as Information Sharing and Analysis Centers (ISAC) presents a proactive factor, enabling organizations to benefit from the experiences of other companies.

Proprietary Information Sources

Threat vendor's act as a source in proffering tactical intelligence, but developing internal proprietary capabilities to acquire consistent information about a specific topic or event source is a valuable endeavor to improve long term value.

Adversary Attribution

Garnering the motivation behind an attack, reason for the attack, and methodology of the attack is significant not only while the attack is in progress, but also afterwards as well, because the upper management will require details relating to it.

Trend Identification

Monitoring attack tendencies offers insight into the forthcoming threats and facilitates planning. Furthermore, prevalence data can be used to identify new trends in the threat landscape and to provide security against emerging threats.

Security Awareness

Security awareness is a mandatory element of any organization's ability to defend against cyber events. Employee education is very crucial. Be it technical or non-technical, security awareness training allows the employees to acquire intelligence about the threats and trends within a global context.

Internal Hunting

Building a hunt team is becoming more popular in the Threat Intelligence landscape. Organizations need to track for rogue insider activity as well as undetected external attacks that have breached the organization's perimeter.

Attacker Tools and Architecture Recommendations

Ascertaining higher level adversary "choke points" that correspond to Tools, Techniques, and Procedures (TTPs) is a major strategic activity that allows IT departments to proactively create a solution.

Operational Component

The operational component includes the following:

Incident Identification

This component mainly focuses on the processing of peripheral attack data from all available sources. By automating this process, internal incidents and external attacks will be identified in time to be of use.

Defensive controls

This component will superlatively mitigate or prevent attacks. Defensive strategies are always in response to particular threats or attacks. Therefore, a clear and complete understanding of the threat environment is vital to mission accomplishment.

Features of a Threat Intelligence Program

A Threat Intelligence Program is sized to fit the requirements of an organization. However, there is plenty of information out there, and the work can swiftly become overpowering. To create a Threat Intelligence program, one needs to:

- Identify sources that delineate and explain the emerging threat landscape
- Document how the sources will be implemented; and
- Allocate roles and responsibilities for Gleaning, analysing, and distributing the information

Going beyond simple event-based data research is a criterion for any expedient Threat Intelligence program. A CTI program will help you create a dependable way to implement the Threat Intelligence data set you amass, so that you can swiftly comprehend and effectually respond to emerging threats.

Implementation of Threat Intelligence Program

The main purpose of implementing a Threat Intelligence program is to help enterprises get awareness of the current and emerging threats and maximize security before an unsolicited event occurs. However, here are some best practices for implementing an expert Threat

Intelligence program.

Build a Strategic Roadmap

A cybersecurity strategic roadmap is a pivotal tool for the whole organization, and a crucial one for the CTI program. The cybersecurity roadmap will help the organization prioritize its investment to fight threats in a way that addresses high risks and ensures its security program aligns with its requirements. However, the Strategic roadmap will:

- Determine gaps in today's cybersecurity practices and competencies.

- Provide a prioritized catalogue of preferred improvements, capabilities, resources and tools as well as a timeline to accomplish the desired state.

- Provide financial investment appraisals to plan and budget effectively to attain cybersecurity goals.

Now let's take a look at some of the significant tasks entailed in creating a strategic roadmap.

Appraise Assets, Adversaries, and Defenses

The first and foremost step in developing a strategic roadmap is to evaluate key assets, adversaries, and defenses. Tasks include:

- Reckoning information assets that need to be shielded and appraising the impact of losing them.

- Determining IT systems that are crucial to business operations, encompassing business applications, infrastructure and operational control systems.

- Discovering potential adversaries and their targets, tactics, tools, techniques and procedures.

Execute a Gap Analysis

The next phase in developing a strategic roadmap is to perform a gap analysis as it highlights which security systems and procedures need enhancement. The most imperative gaps are weak defenses protecting high value information assets. However, those defenses must be reinforced as early as possible.

Although performing a gap analysis is more complicated, it is a vital investment for the Threat Intelligence program. The evaluation procedure bestows the organization a sound basis for ascertaining which improvements are most imperative, and also what Threat Intelligence needs to be gathered and scrutinized.

Draft Investment Priorities

The ultimate step in developing a strategic roadmap

is outlining investment priorities and alternatives. A perfect roadmap allows IT managers to conduct prolific discussions with executive management and draft recommendations in business terms.

Create a Centralized Knowledge Base

A knowledge base or repository is a key tool. Majority of the work performed by security operations center (SOC) analysts, forensics and incident response (IR) teams, and others encompasses correlating data from diverse sources and time periods.

Typically, the information stored should comprise of threat indicators, attack and malware investigation reports, and analytical reports about the attacks detected in the enterprise. Technologies implemented for creating knowledge base could include SharePoint, document management and collaboration systems, databases, and data management tools.

To get the most out of threat data, one can incorporate the knowledge base with SIEMs and other security systems via standard connectors or an application programming interface (API).

Extend Monitoring

The more security information is available, the easier it is for the security professionals to detect and scrutinize attacks.

Track Internal Activities and Traffic

Organizations must be capable enough to accumulate and interconnect log and security event data from security products, servers and network devices. Usually, SIEMs and security analytics apparatuses are deployed for this purpose.

By placing security monitoring systems at strategic choke points in the network, security organizations can monitor lateral traffic within the enterprise. Tools such as full-packet capture systems can be used by the analysts to monitor traffic to and from critical devices. This traffic can unveil attackers endeavouring to escalate credentials, to communicate with C2 (command and control) servers, to identify confidential data and stage it for exfiltration, or to exfiltrate data to external servers.

Monitor External Threats

The security organizations must be organized in tracking external threats via:

- Threat indicator data feeds
- Accurate reports and contextual threat data about attacks and malware
- Flash scrutinizes and news reports of current security events
- Tracking of adversaries on underground websites, web forums and hacker marketplaces

Train Staff or Find a Right Partner

Some of the attributes required to collect and analyse cyber threat information include wide technical expertise, threat research skills, knowledge about how attacks are made, critical thinking, and a mastery of languages. Unfortunately, in the current job market, it is difficult to find expert cyber threat analysts and researchers. In these circumstances, it is best to train existing security staff for these positions.

This process includes finding individuals with technical skills and training them about how to:

- Reconnoitre underground and black market sites
- Customize and package discoveries for diverse intelligence consumers
- Analyze clues and correlate data to create clear pictures of adversaries and their techniques.

Automate Workflows

Automated workflows ensure that CTI is accessible to analysts instantly as context around a threat indicator, without substantial manual exertion. For instance, when a SIEM system gets an alert, it might automatically enquiry the knowledge repository, which would return basic data about the indicator that generated the alert, along with tags allocated to that indicator. If one of the tag is vital for that enterprise, then the SIEM can fag the alert as top priority.

When a SOC team member decides to examine the fagged alert, the SIEM system could also exhibit context about the alert. This will help the analyst to decide whether it should be investigated further, escalated to the IR team, remediated in some way, or ignored. This method is far more effectual and reliable than compelling SOC analysts to enquiry the knowledge base manually each time when they analyse an alert.

Build a Hunt Mission Capability

Most organizations implement Cyber Threat Intelligence only in a reactive manner to help respond to alerts and investigate attacks after they have been recognized. However, a huge number of cutting-edge security teams have adopted a more proactive approach. The main intention of a hunt mission is to proactively anticipate the most possible threats and belligerently search for indicators that might divulge campaigns and attacks in their initial stages.

Threat Hunting Mission should be preceded with an investigation of threats. This analyst-driven process might involve:

- Allotting specific indicators for special investigation and monitoring

- Tagging these indicators so that the hunt team

is notified immediately when it is confronted by the SIEMs or security sensors on the network.

- Following up instantly by pivoting on the early indicator and seeking for related indicators that confirms the occurrence of an attack.

Refine and Improve

An effective and powerful CTI program can never be static. New Adversaries are always evolving and coming up with innovative tools, techniques and procedures. In today's fast paced world, technologies and business initiatives are changing significantly. To stay up-to-date with these fluctuations, repeat the investigations performed when the strategic roadmap was created. However, this includes appraising new adversaries and attacks, performing or updating the gap analysis, and reviewing the CTI requirements.

The success of a CTI program is based on the comprehensive understanding of business objectives, and the building processes that allow the goals to be met. A sturdy Cyber Threat Intelligence program empowers leaders to comprehend the company's footprint on a regular basis and upsurge organizational situational awareness, as the world changes.

Cyber Threat Intelligence Partners

Selecting an ideal Threat Intelligence partner is an important process. Most organizations neither take the time nor follow the proper procedure and therefore, they end up with a partner that isn't the right fit. The degree of collaboration involved in the framework highlights the significance of choosing the right intelligence partner. However, this choice must fit the IT capabilities and business requirements of an individual organization.

Types of Partners

A wide range of product and service vendors pledge to offer certain elements of Threat Intelligence. Generally, they fall into three groups: companies that focus on threat indicators, companies that offer complete Threat Intelligence services, and companies that combine threat indicators with threat data feeds.

Providers of Threat Indicators

A comprehensive array of security vendors and open source projects supply signatures, indicators, and screening rules to control firewalls, IPS/IDS, unified threat management (UTM) systems, antimalware software and other products. In certain cases, the indicators are supplied as raw data; while in others, they are escorted by reputation scores or risk. At the tactical level, Threat indicator feeds are vital for maximizing the efficacy of blocking technologies. Nevertheless, they don't deliver context for incident response.

Providers of Complete Threat Intelligence

Only a small number of firms provide all three types of Threat Intelligence i.e., threat data feeds, validated threat indicators and Strategic Threat Intelligence. The top companies incorporate all three types of intelligence, for instance providing Indicator of compromise (IOCs) that have been authenticated, tagged, and associated to rich context about adversaries. Typical offerings include:

- Authenticated threat indicators with tags
- Comprehensive technical analyses of attack tools
- Detailed research on adversaries, with data amassed from private sources and underground websites.
- In-depth research on existing and emerging threat actors
- Assistance in developing Threat Intelligence requirements
- Threat information custom-made for different audiences at different levels - be it tactical, operational, or strategic.

Providers of Threat Data Feeds

A huge number of security service companies and technology vendors supply threat data feeds. However, this includes accumulation of indicators that have been authenticated and prioritized, plus comprehensive technical investigations of botnets, DDoS attack methods, malware samples and other malevolent tools.

At the operational and tactical levels, Threat data feeds will provide SOC analysts and incident response teams with analytical data about attack tools and basic context about adversaries. Conversely, they rarely deliver information about the tactics or intents of the adversaries.

Threat Intelligence Partner Selection Criteria

Every organization needs to create its own list of criteria for assessing prospective Cyber Threat Intelligence partners. While there are several new companies entering the Cyber Threat Intelligence market, organizations should take a crucial look while choosing their potential partners.

Now, let's explore the key criteria for selecting a Threat Intelligence Partner.

Wide Geographic Reach

Cyber threats differ by geographic region. For instance, if your customers operate internationally, then it's absolutely significant that Threat Intelligence amassed by your partner originates from accumulation points in countries where your customers operate business.

Ease of Integration

Choosing one partner for all of your Cyber Threat Intelligence requirements definitely makes life simple, so does using one API for all of your accredited Threat Intelligence feeds. If your preferred vendor offers a diverse API for each of its licensed Threat Intelligence feeds, then this partly conquers the intention of seeking one partner.

Intelligence Correlation

Even if you choose a single vendor for all of your Threat Intelligence requirements, it doesn't mean that it likely reduces false positives or false negatives. Remember, some potential threats are much harder to categorize as good or bad. In an effort to lessen false negatives and false positives, top Threat Intelligence providers have developed correlation procedures. This procedure, however, will automatically cross reference web reputation feeds against file Threat Intelligence, IP reputation and other intelligence repositories to add contextual awareness and lessen the quantity of unclassified potential threats.

When appraising Threat Intelligence providers, make sure to ask how the vendor is able to correlate threats from numerous feeds in an effort to reduce false negatives and false positives. If they lack this competency, it's in your best interest to find a vendor who possesses this skill.

Intelligence Platform, Knowledge Base and Portal

Infrastructure is a critical facilitator for a CTI operation. Ask the Threat Intelligence providers to:

- Delineate its platform for collecting, investigating, and distributing intelligence.

- Describe or demonstrate the search and retrieval competencies of its knowledge base.

- Allow you experiment with the customer portal to monitor how easy it is to use.

Historical Data and Knowledge

Only few cyberattacks are truly original. Most adversaries reuse existing infrastructure, malware and techniques in new blends, or progress from older methods. Most often, the same adversaries attack companies in the same industry frequently. Due to these reasons, many years of historical data and expert knowledge are invaluable for detecting and scrutinizing the latest attacks.

Therefore, ensure to ask your potential partners when they created their threat knowledge base, and the mediocre tenure of their threat analysts and researchers. Also, ask your potential partner how they maintain the repository and uproot obsolete items.

Range of Intelligence Offering

Make sure your potential Threat Intelligence partner provides all three types of intelligence as mentioned earlier i.e., threat data feeds, validated threat indicators, and strategic Threat Intelligence. Vendors should deliver indicators with tags so that both automated systems and individuals can use to connect Indicators of Compromise to rich context about attacks and adversaries.

A variety of intelligence deliverables should be available with the level of detail, format, and delivery frequency apt for your key users. For instance, intelligence "flashes" for IR and SOC teams, trend reports and higher-level briefings for managers, threat analyses and detailed adversary for IR and forensics teams.

Access to Experts

Ascertain whether your prospective partner offers customers direct access to its experts to answer queries, exchange ideas and elucidate analyses. Also, find out whether these experts pursue formal procedures for collecting, investigating and disseminating intelligence. Furthermore, find out if the managers and analysts at the firm establish integrity with your executives and managers and help validate necessary investments and security initiatives.

Besides evaluating on particular capabilities, don't forget to ask references about the firm's customer service, responsiveness, and eagerness to customize deliverables. Also, find out whether your potential partner has helped clients make utmost use of Threat Intelligence across various levels including tactical, operational, and strategic levels.

Things To Avoid While Choosing A Partner

If you are seeking for a Threat Intelligence partner to deliver complete Cyber Threat Intelligence services, then you should avoid:

- Security services organizations with a regional focus, because threat information needs to be accumulated and evaluated on an international basis.

- Security product organizations, because their services are almost proposed to support the use of their product, not to enhance overall security.

When it comes to threats, the only thing that is constant is change. Threat actors' vary, targets vary, and the methodologies used to deliver threats are also persistently evolving. Having detailed and highly accurate Threat Intelligence is vital to the success of any security product intended to thwart threats. Unfortunately, finding a perfect Threat Intelligence partner is not a frivolous task. No two service providers are the same. The quantity and quality of threat data offered by the service provider varies widely.

The challenges and confrontation you'll face while appraising Threat Intelligence providers are many and compelling. Take the required time to apply the aforementioned selection criteria when evaluating prospective partners for Cyber Threat IntelligenceThreat Intelligence. Choosing the right partner is a critical decision as it can make or break your company and possibly your customers' companies, as well.

Module 12
Use of Cyber Threat
Intelligence in SOC CTAC

Use of Cyber Threat Intelligence in SOC CTAC

As the threat landscape continues to evolve swiftly in both scale and sophistication, the need to safeguard organizations' intellectual property, brand, operations, and shareholder value, along with their customers' data, is more vital. Progressions in the security industry have not kept pace with today's varied set of threat actors. Therefore, organizations find themselves in a position where traditional services and off-the-shelf products are not adequate to address the risk.

Cyber-attacks have not only become more advanced and audacious, but also more varied—from writing malevolent code to stealing intellectual property to lodging political protests. In the current cyber threat landscape, no organization is immune. And cyber security is no longer considered as a technical issue but has emerged as an ultimate business challenge for most enterprises. Progressively, organizations are finding that legacy or disorganized security solutions are no longer acceptable. Furthermore, as the demand grows, many organizations lack the resources in-house to direct, implement and hone cyber security strategies.

In the current digital world, protecting an organization's digital assets is a crucial business concern. As more and more sophisticated attacks occur, defenders are contingent on Cyber Threat Intelligence to get prompt notification of attacks. By scrutinizing the latest indicators of compromise (IOCs), organizations can react upon attacks targeting their industry and respond rapidly before they become victims. Due to the sensitive nature of its work, wide ecosystem of third-party vendors, large number of employees and valuable IP it possesses, the organization should use Threat Intelligence to enhance its overall security.

The ever-fluctuating threatscape of an upsurging digital world challenges the defensive competencies of even the most mature organizations. An effective, well-functioning SOC (Security operations center) can form the heart of active defense and provide a safe environment for the enterprise to deliver on its core strategic goals. SOC is a centralized unit that typically deals with security issues on a technical and organizational level. It is a facility where enterprise information systems such as websites, databases, data centers and servers, applications, desktops, networks and other endpoints are analyzed, assessed, and defended.

The methods and tools used for modern cyber defense are no longer keeping pace with the rapidly changing threats and more sophisticated attacks afflicting our networks. An effectual SOC can allow information security functions to respond quickly, work more cooperatively and share knowledge more effectively. Besides, amalgamation of SOC personnel and security staff greatly limits the time and attention that can be allotted to day-to-day cyber defense.

Currently, organizations are cognizant of the benefits of possessing a well-functioning Security Operations Center. To combat advanced, persistent and multi-stage threats, SOC solutions must move beyond alerts to provide litigable Intelligence. First generation SOCs is prone to focus keenly upon signature-based controls, for example antivirus and intrusion detection systems, enabling organizations to identify "known bad" artifacts related to an attack. The second generation of SOCs presaged the onset of 24x7 operations in acknowledgement that attackers don't close for the day, even if your business does.

The SOC of the future needs to be more effectual to provide an active cyber defense. To make this happen, shared actionable intelligence can be employed across the networks and enclaves in near-real time. For organizations attempting to develop a security operations center for the first time, or those expanding their SOC's coverage or capability, staffing the right people is perhaps the most vital aspect of the people, process, or technology puzzle.

Primary Components of a SOC

- Describe the SOC - Establish the responsibility, mission, and scope of the Security operations center.

- Define the processes - Determine and clearly document the procedures and key templates required to support the SOC.

- Comprehend the environment - Identify the technical domain to be tracked, the "use cases," and the category of data that is received by the SOC.

- Discover the customer - Identify the groups of customers and their interaction with the SOC.

- Staff the SOC - Delineate the operational hours and the requisite staff per shift.

- Manage the events - Classify, allocate, and prioritize events received by the SOC.

- Leveraging ITIL - Comprehend the essential ITIL components to constantly run an effective SOC.

3 Types of Threat Intelligence for SOC Teams

The three types of Cyber Threat Intelligence i.e., tactical, strategic, and operational - provide context, attribution, and action and allow a sturdy foundation for building a successful SOC.

Tactical Threat Intelligence

Tactical Threat Intelligence typically informs what an organization needs to emphasize on while reacting to incidents, utilizing the tools at their disposal. However, this encompasses indicators (such as IP addresses, domains and hashes), artifacts, and other evidence about an existing or emerging threat to assets. SOC analysts implement these artifacts to detect existing or emerging risks and share information about them with other parties to enhance security for all.

Strategic Threat Intelligence

Generally, strategic Threat Intelligence informs how an enterprise protects itself and its overall cyber security posture. Moreover, it provides context and attribution to inform action and defend against the threats' capabilities. At this level, the SOC analysts and SOC leaders scrutinize the TTPs to better understand the adversary intention and tradecraft, to make more informed business decisions, and to assure alignment between their cybersecurity approach and real world risk.

Operational Threat Intelligence

Operational Threat Intelligence is actionable information on particular incoming attacks. Ideally, it applies context and attribution to enable action. Based on collection and analysis of latest raw indicators and other artifacts, updated signatures, rules, and other defensive countermeasures will inform the monitoring infrastructure. At this phase, SOC analysts get alerted of the latest threats in their environment, based on automated updates to their IDS, SIEMs, vulnerability scanners, and other SOC tools.

With three elements in place - context, attribution, and action – Cyber Threat Intelligence can achieve its crucial goals and assist the SOC team in making the right business decisions when it comes to thwarting an attack as well as reducing the time it takes to identify one in action. Furthermore, it can help the SOC team establish the earnestness they need to acquire executive attention and sponsorship.

Application of Cyber Threat Intelligence by SOC Analysts

Advanced Security Operations Centers are using Cyber Threat Intelligence not only to prioritize and validate alerts but also to rapidly identify the specific ones that might signify real threats to the organization. By alleviating the problem and offering instantaneous access to threat context, Cyber Threat Intelligence allows SOC analysts to make faster, better decisions regarding which alerts and alarms should be escalated to Incident Response (IR) teams for detailed investigation and action.

Use Cases
Machine-Based Prioritization

Security information and event management systems

(SIEMs) and security analytics tools provide visibility into thousands (or even millions) of events and threat indicators (such as malicious domains and IP addresses, and archives that may contain malware) identified on an enterprise's network. Most of the alarms, alerts, and events that SOC teams encounter are false positives i.e., threats that will be avoided by existing defenses or threats that won't impact the business. However, by matching alerts and events with Cyber Threat Intelligence, SIEMs and security analytics tools can execute first-cut prioritization at machine speed. This, in general, assuages SOC analysts from the labor-intensive chore of sorting out thousands of low-level and irrelevant alerts each day.

For instance, SOC teams can create SIEM rules that match apparent threat indicators detected on the corporate network (e.g., ports and protocols, domains and IP addresses, file hashes or registry settings) with Threat Intelligence. Simultaneously, Threat Intelligence connects those indicators with threat actors or campaigns that target the enterprise's industry, software applications, infrastructure components or geographical areas of operation. When matches are discovered, the SIEM will automatically upsurge the priority rating of that particular event or alert, ensuring that SOC teams have "keen eyes on" the threats pertinent to their enterprise.

Event and Alert Triage

Though machine-based prioritization can perform

much of the heavy lifting, SOC analysts are still burdened with the arduous tasks of figuring out which alarms and alerts are actually hazardous. Cyber Threat Intelligence can speed up this procedure by bestowing SOC teams with summary threat data that delivers context and "situational awareness." However, this threat data can take the form of summary descriptions and tags that connects individual indicators with threat actors and targets. Also, it can take the form of longer narrative descriptions that position the indicators in the context of campaigns and multi-stage attacks.

For instance, Threat Intelligence can notify the SOC analyst quickly if:

- Malware linked with an alert targets systems or applications present in the enterprise (say POS systems at a retailer or a particular accounting application).

- An IP address on the Internet that was communicated by a system on the network is linked with actors, known to be targeting the enterprise's industry or countries where it operates.

Analysis and Validation

Cyber Threat Intelligence can also help SOC analysts to further evaluate threats and validate events. It allows them to identify which events are likely to pose a significant risk to the enterprise and prioritize those events with the highest possibility for negative impact on the business. Also, Threat Intelligence helps them to determine whether the events are isolated or part of a more complicated targeted attack. "Context" related with alerts can include lists of allied malware families, information about the behavior of malware samples, domains and IP addresses, phishing attacks and other attack techniques.

Intelligence preserved in a cyber-threat knowledge repository can provide additional detail and narratives to the analyst, for instance, attribution of malware or phishing messages to a particular threat actor or group, investigation of the steps implemented in a multi-stage attacks, and suggested options for extenuation. These Cyber Threat Intelligence resources can assist SOC analysts to swiftly assemble evidence to ascertain if alerts and events should be categorized as incidents that pose critical threats to the organization or should be escalated to the IR team for instant in-depth analysis.

Therefore, these use cases signifies that Cyber Threat IntelligenceThreat Intelligence can help SOC analysts to:

- "Shrink the problem" of a devastating number of security alerts, alarms and events.

- Promptly discover alerts associated with pertinent threats to the enterprise.

- Eradicate the inefficiencies of sorting through huge volumes of low-priority or invalid alerts.

- Rapidly assemble and appraise evidence and make better decisions regarding which incidents to escalate.

SOC Analyst Challenges

As the number of alerts, alarms as well as events generated by security tools increases rampantly, SOC analysts find it difficult to determine which ones are most imperative, which require immediate attention, and which are part of campaigns and advanced attacks. SOC analysts must deal with the chore of segregating impactful threats from noise and ascertaining where to focus restricted incident response resources. Some of the most complicated challenges faced by them include:

- Lack of information to isolate invalid, irrelevant or unreliable alerts and alarms from those posing a stern risk to the enterprise.

- The near unfeasibility of analyzing from tens of lakhs to millions of alerts and alarms daily to identify the most significant threats.

Cyber Threat Analysis Cell

A Cyber Threat Analysis Cell (CTAC) is a team

primarily composed of skilled and advanced security analysts organized to discover, deny, disrupt, degrade, and deceive the advanced persistent threat (APT). Its presence presupposes the presence of a routine cybersecurity tracking and incident response competencies, such as a SOC. Cyber Threat Analysis Cell is part of a Security operation center and it depends completely on the SOC capabilities. A SOC offers services to a group of customers referred to as a constituency - a confined set of users, IT assets, sites, networks, and organizations. In order for an enterprise to be considered a Security operation center, it must:

- Provide a mode for constituents to report alleged cyber-security incidents.

- Provide incident handling support and guidance to constituents.

- Distribute incident-related information to constituents as well as external parties.

Operating the Cyber Threat Analysis Cell allows the SOC to be a sophisticated producer and consumer of Cyber Threat Intelligence. While addressing the advanced persistent threat is the crucial concern of a CTAC, its TTPs augment all aspects of a SOC's capabilities. A designated team within the SOC may be regarded as a CTAC, if it regularly performs the following core functions:

- Extraction of IOCs, through a blend of digital artifact analysis, runtime malware implementation, static code examination and reverse engineering, and simulation procedures.

- Regular ingest of Cyber Threat IntelligenceThreat Intelligence updates and reporting from a range of sources.

- Meld of locally derived and externally sourced Threat Intelligence into signatures, analytics and techniques proposed to detect and monitor the APT.

- Advanced incident scrutiny and response support, say digital forensics of memory and hard drive images.

- Dynamic involvement in cyber intelligence threat-sharing groups - generally comprised of other SOCs in an analogous geographic region, analogous supported industries and organizations, or both.

Often, the Cyber Threat Analysis Cell is composed of some of the SOC's most skilled and experienced analysts. The swiftly evolving nature of Advanced Persistent Threat's TTPs often pushes a CTAC to execute the following additional functions:

- Generating and fine-tuning progressive analytics to detect advanced or complicated attack patterns, such as those utilized to detect and monitor the Advanced Persistent Threat in the SOC's SIEM.

- Developing focused, stupendously scoped custom tools that allow the CTAC to detect, monitor, hold, or block the APT at diverse phases of the cyber-attack lifecycle.

- Administering and populating a threat knowledge management capability, enabling SOC analysts to connect incongruent but related adversary activity, indicators, events and artifacts.

- Trending and documenting on incidents and activity accredited to the APT.

- Pursuing for the existence of the APT on tracked networks.

- Honeypotting and other techniques that empower the CTAC to monitor the adversary.

A Cyber Threat Analysis Cell must keenly monitor the myriad threats that exist all over the Internet. Its response activities' are quite defensive in nature and are confined to the scope of systems it is probed to defend. The CTAC should develop a good working relationship with entities authorized to perform cyber analyses and feasibly direct responses against adversaries, such as some categories of law enforcement.

What Does CTAC Provide?

A CTAC produces a cluster of deliverables and artifacts on a regular basis. Some of these deliverables are easily recognized papers or briefings, while others take the form of inputs to an online knowledge repository or updates to tools and technologies implemented by the CTAC. Running a Cyber Threat Analysis Cell provides a huge number of crucial, first-order benefits, and many more second-order impacts that improve cyber security for the organization it serves. However, they are as follows:

Primary Impacts

- Greater confidence in the efficiency and completeness of incident response activities.

- Decreased percentage of APT attacks that are highly successful.

- Deeper threat awareness via direct understanding of adversary TTPs throughout the cyber-attack lifecycle.

- Improved "Situational Awareness" through more informative and detailed threat and incident reporting.

- Increased context and connection between incident activity and mission impact.

Secondary Impacts

- Simpler, quicker SOC service delivery through reduced dependence on external group that execute malware and forensic investigation.

- Higher impact, and focused utilization of cybersecurity resources such as talent, time, funding, etc., on threat-focused hindrance, sensoring, analytics and response capabilities.

- Enhanced self-confidence, emanating from sense of fraternity and harmony with partner SOCs.

- Greater attractions and retention of SOC workforces through extended career development and membership in a first-class capability.

- Improved stakeholder responsiveness thanks to SOC's competencies to eloquent meaning of adversary events in context of operation, and morale in efficiency of incident response activities.

- Considerable savings of exertion by leveraging solutions and Threat Intelligence from partner

SOCs.

- Improved awareness of enterprises threat profile and possible targets of adversary attack.

- Deeper insight into gaps in situational awareness and complementary willpower to fill those gaps.

How Does the CTAC Integrate into IT and Security Ops?

CTAC should work successfully hand in hand with every part of the SOC, and with a number of other stakeholders outside its parent SOC. Even though CTAC, by itself, has certain tools to track and detect the APT, it is heavily dependent on SOC and IT operations in other areas furnished tools for censoring and blocking with analytical response capabilities and responsibilities.

Cyber Threat Analysis Cell (CTAC) as a team is composed of exceptional security analysts organized to detect, deny, disrupt, degrade, and deceive the APT. The existence of CTAC surmises the existence of a routine cyber security monitoring and incident response capability, such as a SOC. A CTAC depends on the potentiality of SOC and it takes the major part in CTAC.

CTAC integrates into IT and Security Ops for Threat Intelligence actionable information that gives early warnings of cyber threats. Security intelligence seeks to collect relevant information for analyzing and synthesizing it into meaningful knowledge. CTAC achieves this in cyber threat landscape with intelligence alert. Intelligence helps in identifying the actors that target organization with Advanced Persistent Threats, providing the insights to prepare or take the required action.

The CTAC can be successful if it works conjointly with every part of the SOC, CTAC enables the organizations to forecast, respond to and remediate threats. However, an organization's focus on positioning teams for success, rich contextual intelligence requires preparation and a base level of capability in order to stretch the value received.

The most common elements of CTAC have been achieved by organizations in their development stage. This includes raw, unfiltered data feeds with CTAC information, tools to anticipate and analyze CTAC. A wide range of accurate and accumulated data integrates into the environment. There are also some senses of accuracy and opportunity related CTAC integration and use.

Specialized expertise, knowledge, and tools developed based on the content searches together create security intelligence with required actionable intelligence. CTAC with required information dimmer the areas of the Internet and hacker communities to construct an overall picture of disparate puzzle pieces of data.

Cyber threats in IT department are crucially observed by CTAC team and following strategies are adopted to minimize the cyber threats:

- Incidents that are focused in nature are linked to a known APT or may be referred to the CTAC for in-depth analysis. The CTAC working notes, activities, recommended follow-up and other analyst communications are listed in the SOC's incident case tracking capability as Case tracker notes for reporting daily or weekly.

- Particularly notable incidents are handled by the CTAC with a proper documentation or demonstration outside the scope captured in the SOC's incident tracking capability. This may be in the form of presentations, written reports, or sometimes both, authored by the CTAC or co-authored by the CTAC. SOC incident responders are known for formal incident write-up which is done monthly or quarterly.

- Short and timely information is the tip to a cyber-threat sharing group within minutes or hours of identifying activity targeted intrusion attempt. The information may be a simple activity like sending email address, subject, and attachment names for a spear phish or URLs to a drive for download, or it may includepreliminary malware analysis, such as callback IP addresses, domains, file hashes, persistence mechanisms, and sample beacon traffic.

- Short form of malware report is usually sent on a weekly or monthly basis and it contains two- to-four-page report with details of indicators and information regarding the detected specimen of malware. Generally stock from malware takes one or two days of productive scrutiny to understand.

- Long-form of malware report is usually sent monthly or quarterly and it contains a three-plus-page report that furnishes detailed indicators and reporting on an observation made on a piece of malware. Generally stems from a deep dive reverse engineering effort that takes several days or weeks to accomplish. Typically, these reports include a full description of the malware sample functionality, any encryption used, and its network protocols used for command and control. It may include additional tools and techniques developed alongside the analysis, such as malware network protocol decoders and ways to unpack or extract encryption keys and other indicators from malware samples within the same family.

- Briefs discussion on the TTPs, intent, activity seen, incidents, etc., stemming from a named adversary or adversary campaign, usually strings together the activities seen from multiple incidents.

Secure researchers and security consultants lead to intelligence formulation. Security administrators and analysts actively work in more technical security oriented roles through which Threat Intelligence would be implemented. For each part of the SOC, the CTAC has a responsibility to furnish timely SA regarding the TTPs, activities, and impacts of adversary activity.

In exchange of information, each section of the SOC must enable the CTAC mission in a different way. The CTAC integration in Security Operation can be explained in the following points:

1. In order to grasp the nature of suspected malware, the CTAC will require an environment to perform fixed decomposition/disassembly and runtime execution/simulation of malware. This environment is solely used by the CTAC, it requires a set of very specialized software that usually is operated on a set of hosts or a small network and is well-confined from all other computing resources. As a result, the

CTAC must be responsible for maintaining and updating the capabilities of the malware with analysis.

2. The CTAC requires a means to track and link attacker activity, campaigns, indicators, events, related malware samples, and correlated PCAP samples over time. Though this capability stands aside from the SOC incident case management system, it still supports the integration. The CTAC is the primary author and curator of content in this database. It may be used and referred by all other analysts in the SOC. The report extracted is termed as a threat knowledge management tool and the report will be taken daily or weekly.

3. It is part of the CTAC to aggregate various indicators like suspicious IP addresses, domains, email addresses, etc. to compromise external cyber Intel reporting and its own malware reverse engineering. These indicator lists are primarily used to generate signatures and other detection content in the SOC tool set (NIDS, SIEM, HIDS, etc.). The indicator list can be done internally or generated from the CTAC threat knowledge management tool.

4. Administration and tuning of sensors and analytic systems, such as IDS and SIEM, are

usually not the duty of the CTAC, but of sensor O&M within the SOC. Sometimes it is most decisive for the CTAC to directly translate knowledge of the adversary into signatures or use cases. In such instances, the signature author in CTAC will likely work with sensor admins to document and operationalize it. This activity is known as Sensing and analytics enhancements, which is usually done weekly or quarterly.

5. The CTAC will observe gaps in its power that cannot be gratified through FOSS or COTS solutions. Especially when the CTAC matures over time and has to deal with unique or foremost threats. Quarantining and observing the adversary, parsing or simulating command and control traffic, or ingesting foreign sources of data into a tool are three examples where custom code may be needed. Custom tools or scripts are spun off on an irregular basis, usually developed very quickly, and don't always reach full maturity before they are no longer required.

Sharing Sensitive Information

The Organizations must frequently balance client's rights and protection of staff from the potential violent/ aggressive behavior of service users. The extent of an organization's information sharing activities with its resources, abilities, and objectives should be steady. Information sharing should be categorized based on the activities. The activity with greater value to an organization and its sharing partners necessitates greater protection. Sharing information must be achieved in a way that does not corrode privacy or adversely impacts freedoms. The span of sharing information needs to adders current and future threats of the organization with a clear target, policy, and operational merit to succeed.

The Organization must identify the types of information that key collaborator is authorized for sharing, the circumstances under which sharing of information is permitted, and those with whom the information should be shared. The staff should be provided with information to face such circumstances to make judgments on how to safely approach such differing situations.

Any information collected must be used fairly and transparently. Adequate risk assessment activity should be carried out for the data's safety and protection marking the rights and priority of workers within the organization. The information must be clearly classified and processed to be simple, clear and made genuinely informative. The intensity of the information must be measured in terms of retention duration of the information and the kind of replies they necessitate, whether the questions are compulsory or voluntary. Required measures should be in place to ensure the security of the personal information. The customer rights should be protected with an appropriate support system, which will help them to complain or find out more about how information will be used.

High-level sketch of SOC monitors are accessed by Major IT and cyber security partners such as security personnel, and partners SOCs. Except for SOC no one will have full particulars on hardware/software version and information on how the Monitoring tap points are protected. IT ops, network administration or the offices of CIO/CISO will access the network map. External organizations such as partner SOCs, with some probable suspensions for extra-sensitive signatures or insider threat indicators will have access to observables, indicators, TTP including IDS signatures and SIEM content.

The authorized Individuals assigned for monitoring IT asset audit records, such as system admins and security personnel takes care of the Audit logs for non-SOC assets. Ideally, all such data should be located entirely in the SOC's enclave. Many SOCs will host a website that may include protected/authenticated precise documents frequently being posted, such as the incident escalation flowchart or network maps. Considering the confidentiality inherent in enterprise-class CND, the SOC is encouraged to provide some particulars on how it executes the CND mission to the constituency.

Sharing information about the types of an approach used without disclosing the "secret sauce" on exactly how it's done will go a long way toward building faith with interested parties. The SOC is advised to share some details with selected boards about its TTPs for spotting external adversaries. This presents a lower risk than sharing details about its insider threat program. Even high-level architecture diagrams are okay to share on a limited basis, so long as device details like IP addresses, host names, and software revisions are detached.

Moreover, when the SOC demonstrates forward-leaning, robust capabilities, it informs users that their actions are indeed being monitored. This may potentially ward off some flagitious activity. The key, though, is not disclosing so much that a malicious user knows how to circumvent monitoring.

The frame work of Sharing Sensitive Information includes the following:

- Monitoring architecture: High-level depiction should be made on how SOC monitors the constituency of Major IT and cybersecurity stakeholders such as constituency executives, security personnel, partner SOCs, and others are listed.

- Monitoring tap points: Full details on how the information should be maintained or deployed with sensors, exact locations of sensor taps and details must be protected.

- Monitoring hardware/ software versions and patch level: Greater internal control must be established for SOC maintenance or deployment sensors.

- Network maps: The consistency of networks such as IT ops, network administration, or the offices of CIO/CISO in the Organizations need to be shaped appropriately for better understanding.

- Vulnerability lists and patch levels: Scan test results with the purview over the vulnerability status of the constituency include sysadmins, ISSMs, or CIO/CISO that should be protected.

- SOC system and monitoring outages: SOC management reporting chain should be structured appropriately and controls must be defined from the CISO or head of IT operations hierarchy.

- Observables, indicators, and TTP including IDS signatures and SIEM content:Partner SOCs or External organizations must have some potential exclusion for extra-sensitive signatures or insider threat indicators.

- Major incidents: Reports must be generated with incident details, including personal and identifiable information, especially for Incidents those are directly above the SOC in its management reporting chain, possibly the CISO, in accordance with legal or statutory reporting requirements with a national SOC

- Incident details: Personally identifiable information appropriate to investigative bodies, such as law enforcement or legal counsel are the incident details

- Incident roll-up metrics and reports

- Constituents of SOC incident escalation CONOPS and flowchart.

- Audit logs for non-SOC assets that includes individually assigned responsibilities for monitoring IT asset, audit records, such as sysadmins and security personnel.

- Raw security events in rare circumstances of selected parties within the consistency support CND monitoring with extensive knowledge of local systems and networks.

Prerequisites To Operate A Cyber Threat Analysis Cell

Below are some of the investments that are needed

to add a CTAC capability to a Security Operation Center.

Foundational Capabilities

For SOCs ready to establish a CTAC, most large tool investments that are needed by a CTAC are as follows:

- A finely-tuned SIEM tool that comprises advanced real-time correlation and the capability to create custom analytics.

- Network IDS sensors capable of custom signature support, and full traffic capture in main places like WAN uplinks, Internet gateways, and firewall boundaries.

- Host defense and sensor suites that encompass AV capabilities.

- An out-of-band SOC enclave network with no trust relationships, with external networks.

Analysis Environment

One of the most vital investment tools required to operate a CTAC is the software and hardware used to support digital media forensics and malware investigation. The CTAC should perform malware investigation on sturdy workstations disconnected from other organizations' networks, while the SOC may choose to process the bulk of its digital forensic artifacts on its existing enclave network. This is conducted predominantly to prevent the inadvertent spread of malware to other

SOC or enterprise systems. The CTAC's static malware investigation capability should include innumerable tools used to unpack, disassemble, decompile, trace, and scrutinize malware samples. Besides, the tools, utilities, and scripts should support:

- Executable unpacking

- Windows Portable Executable (PE) header investigation

- AV scanning

- Report and metadata investigation tools covering formats such as PDF, Microsoft Office and RTF

- Scripting and runtime investigation tools covering languages such as Flash, Java, and JavaScript.

It is always best to incorporate all of these tools into one environment, as CTAC analysts will need to leverage a fusion of these competencies in order to achieve their objectives most effectively.

Threat Knowledge Management

The CTAC distinguishes itself from other cybersecurity groups by its in-depth knowledge of the cyber threat. It must develop a knowledge base about the adversary over time, so that all affiliates of the SOC, existing or new, can directly leverage. However, this knowledge base should:

- Be organized, such that antique artifacts and information can be recovered rapidly.

- Be scalable, enabling the SOC to build up massive amounts of information and correlated contextual data over time, monitoring dozens to hundreds of adversaries, tracking hundreds of thousands of indicators, and TBs of digital artifacts.

- Allow analysts to draw links between pertinent items, enabling them to cross reference or "pivot" amongst them.

- Support incessant pruning of old or erroneous information.

- Support SOC analysts to easily refer back to authentic reporting for context and understanding.

The diverse SOCs implement diverse tactics to satiate these requirements, based on the quantity of data they desire to store and the number of analysts who will utilize it. Also, the cost of setting-up a threat knowledge management tool is very tool-specific. Furthermore, there is an ongoing labor charge associated with importing and managing the knowledge repository within the tool.

Remote Incident Response

Indicator sweeping tools and remote incident response is a vital facilitator for hunting for the existence of the adversary on enterprise systems and networks. They permit the SOC to execute tasks such as seeking for a Windows or remotely imaging a system's memory. Registry setting connected with a part of malware is a facility that can be a huge advantage to the CTAC, both in terms of shrinking response time and conducting tasks across hundreds of hosts instantaneously. Some SOCs may analyze and triage costs associated with the numerous host-based protections at their disposal, specifically with regard to scale and sustainability.

People

One of the major challenges to operating a CTAC is identifying and retaining qualified staff. This is already a great challenge for anyone supervising a SOC, but sternly so for the CTAC. In a viciously competitive labor market, keeping all of those positions occupied can be an arduous task, exclusively for SOCs that involve extensive background checks and clearance requirements, such as those in government and certain areas of industry. CTAC analysts with knowledge of the SOC's detection apparatuses should be competent enough to create signatures for those tools based on cyber intelligence they deal with.

Physical Space

Evaluating space requirements for a CTAC within a Security Operation Center is comparatively straightforward. Many additional SOC cubicles and workstations are needed, for a CTAC to operate successfully. Preferably, each section of the SOC (including the CTAC) will have its own clustered cubicle. The cubicles used by the CTAC are most likely the ones implemented by Tier 2 analysts, with ample room to accommodate manifold monitors, possibly a malware investigations or forensics workstation, the analysts' normal supplement of workstations, related power and network cabling and a small assortment of technical books. Furthermore, some members of the CTAC will need workspace for maintaining digital forensic artifacts, and paper copy of various cyber intelligence reporting. Also, this space must accommodate specific forensics equipment, such as flyaway kits, imagers, and media safes.

Glossary

Index of Tables

Index of Figures

Lightning Source UK Ltd.
Milton Keynes UK
UKHW050327010421
381281UK00015B/160